Breaking the Habit of Dating Your Past

Breaking the habit of
DATING YOUR PAST

A practical strategy to propel you on your journey to true love

TAMARA LEERSON

Copyright © by Tamara Leerson 2019, 2022
Published in Australia by Tamara Leerson 2019
Revised edition 2022

All rights reserved. No part of this book may be reproduced by any mechanical, photographic or electronic process, or in the form of phonographic recording; nor may it be stored in a retrieval system, transmitted, or otherwise be copied for public or private use – other than for "fair use" as brief quotations embodied in articles and reviews without prior written permission of the publisher.

Disclaimer: The author of this book does not dispense medical advice or prescribe the use of any technique as a form of treatment for physical, mental, emotional or medical problems without the advice of a qualified physician, directly or indirectly. The remedies, approaches, concepts and techniques described herein are of the nature of general comment only and are not meant to supplement, or be a substitute for, professional medical care or treatment. While all attempts have been made to verify information provided in this publication, the author assumes no responsibility for errors, omissions or contrary interpretation of the subject matter whatsoever under any condition or circumstances. In the event you use any of the information in this book for yourself, the author and the publisher assume no responsibility for your actions. It is recommended that the reader obtain his or her own independent advice from a qualified healthcare professional.

Disclaimer: Parts of this book are fiction. Names, characters, businesses, places, events and incidents either are the products of the author's imagination or used in a fictitious manner. Any resemblance to actual persons, living or dead, or actual events is purely coincidental. The Author asserts the Authors's Moral Rights in this work throughout the world without waver.

The author's experiences are noted with "I". Recreated events, locales and conversations are from memories of those instances. In order to maintain anonymity in some instances, the names of individuals, the places as well as identifying characteristics and details have been changed.

Australian English is the editing language.

Editor: Stephanie Jaehrling

Typeset and cover over layout by BookPOD. Cover image by Shutterstock.

ISBN: 978-0-6485485-0-8 (pbk) 978-0-6485485-1-5 (e-book)

www.tamleerson.com

 A catalogue record for this book is available from the National Library of Australia

DEDICATION

To my children Candice and Dean, who have been my greatest teachers.
To my mother, for her constant support.

CONTENTS

Introduction 9

PART ONE

Chapter 1: Awareness 13
    The first sign: He tells you what you need to know 14
    The second sign: Your reaction 17
    The third sign: Your inner voice 19
    The fourth sign: The universe 21
    The fifth sign: Your body 23
    The first sign as a life lesson 25
    Highlights 28
    The five signs summary 29
    Reflections 30

Chapter 2: Filtering 31
    The nine filtering patterns 32
    The five signs and our filtering 46
    The job interview 48
    Filtering and the signs: Online dating 50
    Highlights 55
    The nine filtering patterns summary 57
    Reflections 59

Chapter 3: History 61
    Dating the family 61
    The narcissist 64
    Gaslighting 73
    Love 73
    Empower yourself 75

Highlights 79
Reflections 81
End of relationship pick-me-ups! 82
End of Part 1 85

PART TWO

Chapter 4: Transformation 89
  Your first steps 90
  Justified resentment 95
  Certainty 99
  Perceptions 102
  Beliefs 107
  Disappointment 112
  Highlights 124
  Reflections 125
  Moonlight affirmations 126

Chapter 5: Evolving 127
  Your first steps 128
  Wishing them bad 133
  Short-term pleasure 138
  Highlights 146
  Reflections 147
  Moonlight affirmations 148

Chapter 6: Change 149
  Your first steps 150
  Wheat and dairy 154
  A clear mind 158
  Grow your own 162
  Highlights 166
  Reflections 167
  Moonlight affirmations 168

Chapter 7: Accelerate 169
   Your first steps 170
   Intuition 175
   Gratitude 177
   Be love 179
   Higher purpose 183
   Our highest state 187
   Highlights 192
   Reflections 193
   Moonlight affirmations 194
   End of Part 2 195

PART THREE

Chapter 8: Manifesting 199
   Soulmates and life partners 199
   Your list 204
   Manifesting notes 213
   Meditation 215
   Manifesting consciousness 218
Conclusion 223
   Highlights 225
   Reflections 227
   Moonlight affirmations 228
   Reminder 229
Further reading 231
Bibliography 233
Acknowledgements 237
   Contact information 239

INTRODUCTION

This book is a compilation of my life's study, including my observations as a healer, as a facilitator, as a friend and as a mother.

This book, although written for the female perspective, applies to other relationship perspectives and genders. You will see boyfriend, partner or husband, interspersed in the text, adjust in your mind to the term you prefer best.

This book could be titled "breaking the habit of repeating your past", as the writings can be applied across your entire life. Use the mantra, "They tell you what you need to know", to remind yourself that you've heard what you need to know to evaluate whether to allow this person into your life. Whether they are a tradesperson, a boyfriend, a lover, or a friend. Remember, everyone tells you who they are.

Please know the universe is on your side, guiding you with signs and messages, calling you to uplift to a higher life, a higher path.

Know that love, happiness and joy are your birthright.

My hope for you is that this book unlocks the door to the love, joy and happiness that lie within you and propels you on your journey to true love.

Much love, Tam.

PART ONE

CHAPTER 1

AWARENESS

"A wise woman wishes to be no one's enemy; a wise woman refuses to be anyone's victim."
— Maya Angelou

Awareness is your greatest gift, rising up from that painful place, the breakup. Words, some version of, you've heard before: "It's not you, it's me", "I'm not ready for a relationship", "I want to focus on my career", are painful reminders that you have chosen wrong – once again.

But for others awareness comes from escaping yet another toxic relationship, infused with gambling, alcohol, substance abuse, physical, mental or emotional abuse, just to name a few. An all too familiar thread weaving its way through each relationship.

An analysis of the past makes you think back, wondering how yet again you ignored the signs. You knew they were there, but you were missing the knowledge that each sign was a message specific to you. As well as the understanding of why you ignored each sign, leading you to where you are now, once again repeating the past.

There are five signs which help reveal whether you are

dating your past and nine filtering patterns as to why you've ignored the signs. These five signs and nine filtering patterns are now your tools to help free you from the past.

The five signs

The system of the five signs is simple. Each sign builds upon the last, and each brings greater clarity as to whether this relationship is just another version of you dating your past.

The five signs are:

The first sign: He tells you what you need to know.

The second sign: Your reaction.

The third sign: Your inner voice.

The fourth sign: The universe.

The fifth sign: Your body.

Part one of this book teaches you the five signs and how you filter and dilute the message of each sign – why you miss or ignore the red flags. Part two is dedicated to shifting the patterns and breaking the habits causing you to repeat the past, which leads into part three which is dedicated to manifesting a new beginning, your new beginning, the future you have been waiting for.

The first sign: He tells you what you need to know

He tells you what you need to know is your first sign revealing your future life with him. He reveals the first sign, through his life stories. Casual chatting over dinner, over coffee, or during walks in the park, allows his life stories to unfold.

This sign also contains the clue to the life lessons you will learn in your relationship with him as well as revealing the method through which you will learn those life lessons. The method being, whether via a feather duster, a big stick or a sledgehammer (the easy way, the more difficult, and the hard way).

You will see in this book "he tells you what you need to know" shortened to "his warning". Those of you who have encountered addicted or abusive husbands, partners and boyfriends, will know that those early signs are indeed your warning. When he tells you what you need to know, and it involves abuse or coercive control, then it is your warning that the sledgehammer is coming into your life, smashing apart your mental and emotional happiness.

What if he doesn't share?

Telling you nothing is telling you something. If he is unwilling to share, or he is unable to acknowledge one fault, or enlighten you with his ex's complaints about him, then he is telling you what you need to know. If details are missing, honesty is missing, and then you have his warning about your future through what he is not revealing.

He is repeating his past

Your job as the owner of your life is to listen out for his repeating patterns. He is unwinding and repeating his past just as you are. Yes, we think he is perfect when we first meet him. **But his repeating patterns become your repeating patterns when you allow him into your life.**

Life situations that you may never have encountered before, such as drugs, addiction, family disputes, gambling, violence – these things might be normal for him. And because you let him into your life, his past becomes your future.

But the difference between "his" repeating past and "your" repeating past is that you wish for change. You realise that deeply ingrained patterns have been creating your life and you now wish to live an empowered life where happiness and joyful relationships are your new normal.

Ruby

When Ruby met Luke, they talked non-stop. They laughed, they clicked, and started seeing each other. Luke told her that he didn't want a serious relationship. He also told her that he had been looking for "that special someone", but hadn't been able to find her. Ruby latched onto his words. She could be that special someone!

But as the weeks and months went on, Luke became distant, phoning erratically, leaving days between responding to texts. But Ruby didn't give up; she waited for his call or his text. When they were together they had a great time. She couldn't understand what was wrong.

When Ruby first met Luke, he told her what she needed to know: he didn't want a serious relationship. Ruby's pattern of repeating the past was to date guys who would not commit. Luke told her straight up, he was not going to commit, he didn't want a serious relationship, but she ignored his words and repeated her past, once again.

Choose the feather duster way of learning. Believe him when he speaks.

The second sign: Your reaction

When he tells you what you need to know, whether it is a pattern you have been repeating, such as bringing in guys who will not commit, dating a narcissist or dating guys with substance abuse problems, or whatever your pattern is, your immediate reaction to hearing what you need to know is your second sign.

Your reaction is your internal guide, informing you to be on alert. Shock is the most common reaction and it is your sign to stop and evaluate whether to let him into your life. Your reaction may also be stunned, shaken, repulsed, and disbelief after hearing what you need to know.

The second sign is your internal message to be aware that not only is your past repeating, but that his past may be coming into your future.

Chelsea

Chelsea met Mark at her local bar. She was newly single and hated being alone. Mark was funny, positive and forward-thinking. He also had an investment portfolio and a good job. She couldn't believe her luck; Mark ticked all her boxes. He was potential husband material.

At a restaurant, on their second date, Mark wasn't happy with the food. He picked on every part of the dish, commenting on the taste, the arrangement and where the meat was sourced. Chelsea could see the people around them looking up from their food. Mark called the waiter over and demanded a replacement. The waiter apologised, and organised a replacement and a complimentary dessert. Chelsea was happy with the waiters response, but Mark seemed unimpressed. As they left, he said just loud enough to be overheard by the waiter and customers "I should call his boss, he should be sacked."

Chelsea was shocked. The waiter looked distressed. But Mark leant forward and kissed her hand. He made a sad face. Her heart melted and she soon forgot the restaurant commotion.

Six months later, it was Christmas and Chelsea and Mark drove to her family's annual party. They drove in her car, as Mark's was in for repair. On the way, Mark pointed out which road she should take, what lane she should be in, and said "watch out" as if every driver was a potential threat. Chelsea grew nervous by the minute and missed the freeway exit to her parents' house.

Mark slammed his hand down on the dash. He told her to pull over and said, "just typical of you to do that. You can't get anything right, can you? Can you!" She felt his stare cut right through her. These days barely a week went by that he didn't put her down.

Mark gave Chelsea his warning when she met him. He told her what she needed to know. He puts people down. Chelsea ignored her shocked reaction at the restaurant.

Your shock, horror or other negative emotion is your second sign. It shows you the gravity of what you have just heard. It is your internal guidance, telling you to be on alert.

Your reaction to "he tells you what you need to know" is your second sign. It warns you what to expect in your relationship with him, it tells you what is coming into your life.

When you ignore your shock, his "brand" or version of his past is coming into your future.

The third sign: Your inner voice

Your mind talks to you with its never-ending chatter. But beyond that chatter is your inner voice, the small voice within you which whispers to you. It glides through your mind on occasions so fast, that you don't register its importance. Be alert to its message; it will tell you when something is not right.

When on a date and you hear "what you need to know", and it may shock you, in that moment your inner voice may speak: "I would never do that."

Your inner voice is warning you that your values have been violated. Your values guide you on what is right and wrong.

Your inner voice adds weight to the signs you have already felt and heard. It is your message to know whether to allow him into your life. It is your warning sign that not only is your past repeating but that his past is coming into your future. It is your third sign.

Melissa

Melissa met Paul at a sporting fundraiser. Paul was a member of the committee and worked hard organising events, running raffles and making sure the teams had their equipment. Everyone at the club only had praise for him. Melissa felt that she had met "the one".

On their third date, Paul told Melissa about an incident from many years before. Paul revealed that he no longer saw his brother after accusing him of making a pass at his then girlfriend. Paul's brother denied it and an argument followed, resulting in Paul punching his brother and kicking him out.

Melissa was shocked. She thought to herself, "I would never do that." She had a sister; they would never allow things to escalate to a point where they stopped speaking to one another, and violence just wasn't part of their family. Although shocked, Melissa listened to his justifications and decided that this one incident was something from his past.

To celebrate their one-year anniversary they drove down the coast and stayed at a beach resort. Whilst there, they became friendly with another couple, Sue and Brad. Sue had hurt her foot on some coral and suggested that evening that Melissa dance with Brad, since Paul did not want to dance and she couldn't. Brad was a great dancer and before long, the dance floor was full, glasses were clinking and everyone was happy.

At the end of the evening, back in their room, Melissa jumped in the shower. When she came out, Paul was pacing in front of the bed. Seeing her, Paul lunged, his finger pointing in her face, "You made me look like a fool, I could see what you were doing dancing with Brad." Paul grabbed Melissa, pinning her against the wall he continued his verbal abuse. Melissa felt the cold wall against her back. She saw the anger in his eyes; she dared not speak.

When Melissa met Paul, he told her what she needed to know. He gave her his warning. He becomes violent when jealous. Melissa ignored her shock, she ignored her inner voice, her internal alert, telling her that this man does not share her values.

When you meet someone and you hear what you need to know, and you react with shock or horror, as well as hearing your inner voice, be on alert. It is your third sign to know you are repeating your past and that his past will be your future.

When your inner self speaks, hear its message.

The fourth sign: The universe

Signs from the universe can include random messages from friends, songs or talkback on the radio as well as sudden conversations with people you hardly know, all telling you the same thing. Even the jewellery from your boyfriend or partner is a sign. Stones falling out, or the jewellery breaking or going missing, are all signs from the universe.

Have you ever had random people tell you the same answer to a question you've asked silently to yourself? Do not discount this as a coincidence. There are no coincidences. The universe is ordered. Nothing is random, or by chance. If you realise that, you will understand the signs from the universe are all around you.

When your new partner turns up in the same career, driving the same car, or having the same random physical similarities as a previous partner, know that you are receiving a sign. We do not realise the universe has a sense of humour and these similarities can be signs that we are dating the same person.

We often forget to get quiet and tune into our inner knowing. Ask, "What am I missing here? Is there something I need to know?" If you are not sure what messages you are receiving from the universe, ask for a clearer sign. The key to receiving messages is not to be on alert and looking for them. Just ask the question and be assured the answer "will appear" in the hours or days following.

Alice

Alice met James at a bar. James told her he had saved a man who was being beaten up in a laneway one night. He was the guy his friends called upon when they were in trouble. His stories captivated her and she was instantly attracted to him. He was a real-life hero.

On their third date, Alice asked James about his previous relationship. James said his last girlfriend spied on him constantly, taking his phone and reading his messages. She nagged and quizzed him every time he went out. He ended up cheating on her, just to get back at her for her mistrust.

Alice was shocked. Cheating for revenge. Her inner voice spoke: "I would never do that." But Alice ignored her shock and her inner voice. She listened to James's explanation, that she had driven him to it, and decided that James's ex sounded crazy and controlling. Alice filed his cheating story as something from his past. Besides, James was amazing; he was a real-life hero.

One afternoon, Alice bumped into James's aunty at a shopping mall. Randomly, she said that James had a bad temper. Alice was shocked; this was the last thing she expected his aunty to say.

Six months later, James moved in with Alice. Life seemed great, but as time went on, James started going out without her, often not coming home until morning.

Soon Alice found herself checking James's phone, until one night he caught her. He grabbed her phone and kicked it, breaking it. He walked out, returning several days later. Alice heard the news she was dreading. He told her, "Now you have a reason to check my phone. She's better than you anyway."

Alice had ignored the signs. James had told her his values were different from hers; she would never cheat on a boyfriend and never for revenge. She ignored her shock and her inner voice. Bumping into his aunty, the universe gave Alice a further sign.

Know that the universe is on your side, that seemingly random coincidences and messages are not random.

Someone better is out there, someone who will love you and uplift you in every area of your life.

The fifth sign: Your body

Your body hears what your conscious mind ignores. It is like an antenna picking up signals from the world around you. Some people get a "knowing". They know the next step, or they know this guy isn't right for them. They cannot articulate why they know, they just know. This knowing is your gut instinct, your body's internal guidance system.

Your body is on your side, and will attempt to get your attention through symptoms it may develop. [1]Henry Maudsley, an English psychiatrist, said in his book, *The Pathology of Mind* (1895), "The sorrow which has no vent in tears may make other organs weep."

The mind will decide in response to something it hears or sees, "that's weird" or "that was strange". This labelling of stories as weird and strange causes you to ignore behaviour, file it away in the back of your mind and forget about it.

Ask yourself questions when you come upon behaviour you have never encountered. Ask, "Would I do that? Would I say that? Is that normal behaviour?" Do not allow yourself to file away strange behaviour. Tune into your body and ask, what is it I need to know?

Your body is where you live. The better you know it, the better you can support it. It is your best friend and it is always with you. Love and nourish your body. Feed it fresh food and water; feed it real food. Your body is home to your gut instinct, your intuition. Look after it and allow it to do its job, to pick up the warnings that your mind ignores.

Create a new habit of tuning into your body. With each twinge, ting, feeling of stress or uneasiness, sit quietly, take some deep breaths and ask: "What is it I need to know? What are you trying to tell me?" If the answer comes straightaway, then great, but sometimes you just need to jump in the shower or go for a run to free your mind to allow the answer to come through.

---

1   Acknowledging Marisa Peer.

Olivia

Olivia developed shortness of breath during her former relationship. It was only after she broke up with her boyfriend that she realised her symptoms occurred when he put her down. He would say things like, "You don't know what you are talking about", or "That's a stupid thing to say." She ignored his put-downs, but her body never did.

We think of our body as separate from ourselves; we forget that our body is listening to all the mind hears and says. We think when our body is ill or in pain that it is trying to sabotage us, but often it is giving us a message. Next time you develop symptoms, ask your body: "What are you trying to tell me? What am I ignoring?"

Your body is on your side. It is your one true friend. Be kind to it; hear its message.

The first sign as a life lesson

Sometimes you might wonder, what if he hasn't told me anything bad. You've heard no deal breakers, no red flags. One question you can ask is: "What would your ex say was the reason you broke up?", or "What would your ex say was your worst aspect?" And if you still receive no deal breakers or red flags, then ask yourself what are the life lessons I've heard.

Did he tell you he's never been in love before, that he has trouble with commitment. Listen out for the life lessons, and ask yourself how you can learn these lessons through other areas of your life.

Life lessons are part of relationships and all relationship

types. What we are aiming to achieve in this book, is to allow life lessons to unfold via the feather duster. You get the message, tune in to your inner wisdom and choose your path of action.

You don't need the universe to hit you over the head with a big stick, and then a bigger stick, and finally the sledgehammer, to wake you up, to stand in your power and return to love.

Elena

Elena was on her second date when she asked Rick, "What would your ex say was the reason that you broke up?" He said to her, "She felt I spent too much time fixing my house, that I could never finish anything, that I could never commit."

Elena knew she was hearing what she needed to know. Commitment was her red flag. She had heard it before from ex-boyfriends when breaking up.

I asked Elena where commitment had been a theme in her life. How could she move forward and use commitment to serve her? Where had she given up committing to a job or project, so that she could stop bringing in boyfriends to teach her about commitment?

She thought about her life; she had always wanted to be a yoga instructor, but never had the courage to take the leap to start the teacher training.

When you eliminate learning lessons via the sledgehammer, you can bring in boyfriends who will grow and learn with you.

Brianna

Brianna met Nathan at a bar. She was 24 and he was 28. Tall and handsome, he looked perfect. He wandered over to where she was sitting and immediately they clicked. He played basketball. She used to coach junior basketball.

His surname was familiar; his cousin played in the national league. Brianna asked whether his goal was to also play in the national league. He said he was trying. He then took a deep breath and said he was also trying rugby, having taken it up these past six months.

Brianna went on alert. "Trying" – it was all too familiar to her. She had given up on playing basketball, not having faith in her abilities. She gave up coaching after a run-in with another coach. She was trying a career elsewhere.

Brianna sat at the bar with her life flashing before her. She realised that all she did was try things. Her habit was to give up when the first obstacle appeared. She realised she had heard a sign. She needed to give up her fear of failure. She didn't need to bring Nathan into her life to teach her how to stop trying and give up when things became hard. Nathan was her sign, that she was manifesting her past.

Nathan could not have known he was telling Brianna what she needed to know. His simple, unimportant word, "trying", was the trigger Brianna needed to stop manifesting her fears, and bring forward a partner based on a higher value, love.

Highlights

- He tells you what you need to know. Sometimes on the first or second date, and other times it unfolds in the weeks that follow.

- Casual chatting unfolds his stories which contain the clues to whether you are repeating the past.

- The signs reveal to you the patterns you have been repeating throughout your life, the life lessons you have been avoiding.

- When listening to his stories, is there a small incident involving violence? Know that you are hearing a sign about your future life with him.

- Did one of his stories shock you? Did you hear your inner voice say, "I would never do that"; these are signs that your values have been violated.

- Our body is listening to his warning, even when we ignore it.

- When he tells you what you need to know, those words he said which shocked you, where your inner voice spoke, and where you received other signs, his past coming into your life. Whether the following months, or the following years, it's coming in.

- If things don't add up, if he's avoiding showing you his true self, what he is not telling you is telling you something.

- You find your happiness by living congruently with your values.

- Know you can learn your life lessons easily. You don't need the sledgehammer anymore.

The five signs summary

He tells you what you need to know

- He tells you what you need to know. Does he bring simple life lessons where you can both grow together as a couple? Or is he bringing lessons learnt through pain and, more importantly, through your suffering?

Your reaction

- Your reaction: You may be shocked, stunned, shaken, repulsed, in disbelief after hearing what you need to know (his warning). Have your values been violated?

Your inner voice

- Did you say to yourself, "I would never do that", or something similar? Have your values been violated? What work has he done to change himself? Are you filing his stories away as strange, weird?

The universe

- Has someone randomly warned you? Have you turned on the radio just at the time when they are discussing something relevant to your new date? Listen and watch out for signs from the universe. Does he work in the same industry, drive the same car or have the same sporting hobbies as previous partners/boyfriends?

Your body

- How is your body reacting? What is your gut telling you? Have you developed symptoms since meeting him? How are you sleeping?

~ Reflections ~

Look back over your dating life.

- Where were you told what you needed to know?
- Do you remember shock, horror or disbelief that you ignored?
- When did you ignore your inner voice?
- How often did you lose or have your jewellery break?
- What were the signs the universe gave you?

After-date questions:

- Did you hear what you needed to know?
- Has violence shown up in any of his stories?
- Did you hear the life lesson you will learn in a relationship with him?
- Do his values align with yours?
- How have you slept since meeting him?
- Do you suddenly have anxiety after speaking or thinking about him?

Values

Your values are what you believe to be important to the way in which you live, you work and you love. They are the principles and standards that you hold yourself accountable to. When you are out of alignment with your values, you are more likely to experience unhappiness.

What are your values?

CHAPTER 2

FILTERING

> "Between thinking and seeing, there
> is a place called knowing."
> — Caroline Myss

A barrier we face to hearing the signs and why we miss and ignore the red flags is how we filter his stories.

Filtering is what we do when we selectively hear what he is saying, focusing on his good points and ignoring his bad, ignoring the signs. We filter his stories in two ways: through our conscious mind and through our unconscious beliefs. With awareness you can help release your conscious mind filtering.

When listening to his stories, if he tells you he beat his last three partners because they dared to question him, or if he tells you that he has embezzled millions of dollars, you are most likely out the door before the entrée has arrived.

But when you repeat the past, whether your past is to date embezzlers or abusive partners, no matter how loud and obvious that first sign is you will ignore it. You filter his message and dilute his warning.

In this chapter, we will look at our conscious mind filtering.

There are nine filtering patterns.

The nine filtering patterns

The first filtering pattern: Ticking boxes

The second filtering pattern: Seduced by his stories

The third filtering pattern: Honesty

The fourth filtering pattern: The past

The fifth filtering pattern: His ex's fault

The sixth filtering pattern: Good day

The seventh filtering pattern: Your values

The eighth filtering pattern: Rushing in

The ninth filtering pattern: Changing him

The nine filtering patterns

The first filtering pattern: Ticking boxes

"Ticking boxes" is a habit which causes us to think he is "the one" – after only one date! This is because one of his stories has matched with something on our "ticked boxes" list. We all have our own individual list that contains our "must haves", along with the things we've always wanted in a husband, boyfriend or partner.

Your ticked boxes list might include: that he comes from a loving family, that he is financially secure, he exercises, he has a sense of humour, he likes animals, he eats healthily, etc. When you meet a guy who matches with your ticked boxes list, it puts you on a high and you start visualising the future. You block out his faults. You hear what you want to hear and you develop "dating blindness". You ignore the signs, his warning about your future, and you repeat your past.

Have you ever walked away from meeting someone and asked yourself, "Why did I say that?" There seems to be a "truth serum" operating on those early dates, which makes us blindly honest. We reveal details from our past that we usually keep hidden.

We need to make sure on those early dates that we are not focusing on our ticked boxes list, and that we hear the signs whilst the truth serum is operating.

What signs have you ignored to get your ticked boxes list?

The second filtering pattern: Seduced by his stories

Another reason we can ignore the signs is that he seduces us with his stories. He casts himself as the hero, the victim or the joker, and so we idolise, sympathise or trivialise with him. His character takes us on an adventure, and we miss his warning.

When he shows up as the hero, we start idolising him. We have grown up with the hero's journey. We see it in the movies, in books and on TV. His story about the hero taps into a primal part of our inner self, our own desire to be the hero, or our own need for rescuing.

It is the same with the victim. The victim archetype resonates deeply with us. We have our own painful life story.

When we hear his victim story we resonate with empathy and compassion.

The joker is the life of the party. He appears charismatic, loved by all. We love him and we love his antics. In being the joker, he resonates with that part of us that desires to be free, to speak and do whatever we want. His stories captivate us and we miss hearing what we need to know.

When you arrive home from a date, ask yourself, "Has he just taken me on a journey? Am I captivated by his story? Have I missed the gravity of what he has said because I am resonating with the character in his story? Am I wishing I were like him? And, if I bring him into my life, is he fulfilling some part within me that I am missing within myself?"

Beware! His stories will enthral you and cause you to miss his warning. He uses those stories to resonate with you, to attract you. Pay attention if he is showing up as the hero, the victim or the joker.

If he is seducing you with his stories and diverting you from the signs, then your past will repeat and his past is coming into your life.

The third filtering pattern: Honesty

We value honesty in a relationship and this is important. When we hear him speak openly about his past, we admire him for telling the truth. We respect him for exposing his weaknesses. Honesty exposes our vulnerability and creates a connection.

But admiring his honesty can divert us from hearing what we need to know. We think he is exaggerating his faults, just as we can do ourselves with our weight and appearance. But what he is doing is telling us the truth. Hear his story. He is warning you. His past is coming into your future.

Stop admiring him for his honesty and shift your focus. Is he bringing with him simple life lessons that you can grow your relationship on, or do his words contain a warning that his past will be your future?

Know that the universe has drawn his honesty about his negative past out of him. His revelations are a clue to the path your relationship will take. Focus on what he is revealing. Honesty is a given, not a privilege in a relationship.

Beware of admiring him for his honesty, ignoring the signs and missing the warning within his words.

The fourth filtering pattern: The past

Another reason we can ignore the signs is that his stories are about past mistakes. We assume that he has learnt and grown from the past. We decide that he would not be revealing troubling personal details if his past were not over. But these past stories are our future reality and they contain his warning, telling us what we need to know.

We know the effort required to change. We know what we have done to move on from our past. Therefore, when he talks about his negative past, we need to hear the effort he has made to change.

What decisions did he make after going through his experiences? How has he grown and changed? What courses or therapies has he done? What vision of his future self does he have? Is he moving towards his life purpose?

Unless he has learnt clear lessons from his past and has made life changes, we are at risk of allowing his past into our future. If we decide that the events of his past were a one-off, then we can ignore the signs and miss the gravity in his words.

When we assume his past is in the past, we can miss his message that his negative past is coming into our future.

The fifth filtering pattern: His ex's fault

We can also ignore the signs when he blames his ex for his past behaviour. He tells us she complained all the time, she was clingy, she spent too much, she drank, she was anxious all the time or she was depressed. He tells us he was the poor innocent soul who had to put up with her. We have sympathy for him because he describes her in such a way that makes her out to be a total psycho, out-of-control bitch!

But, what we do not realise is that he has just enacted the first rule of storytelling. Create sympathy for the main character. We tell ourselves we are not like his ex. We are nice, we have a different personality. He will not have that trouble with us, we affirm to ourselves.

When he blames his ex for all his problems, then you know that he takes no responsibility for his part in what happened. In his eyes, she was the problem, not him. He has no desire to change. His past will be your future.

Get curious! Why was his ex depressed? Why did she have a breakdown? Why does she have anxiety and how did she end up that way? The answers are your clues. The clues are an insight into your future, a future that has you ending up depressed, anxious and having a nervous breakdown, just like her.

When he tells you that she caused all their problems, you have his warning that his past will show up in your future.

The sixth filtering pattern: Good day

On those early dates we see him on a good day. We judge and filter his stories based on that day. That is a day without problems, without children crying, without you inconveniencing him or without you having a bad day and telling him off for no reason.

You need to know how he handles a bad day. How does he react when faced with a challenge? When under stress, what is his response? Is he looking for a solution or does he look for someone to blame? Does he say we can work this out, or does he attack you and your loved ones? Does he put you down on a bad day? Does he revert to sarcasm?

How does he handle stress at work? Does he change jobs often? Does he walk out on meetings? Does he tell you how bad his boss is? How many "bad bosses" has he had? Why is he attracting them?

How does he act around his family? Does he revert to being "the child"? Does he shout and put his parents and siblings down? Does he treat them like slaves? Does he have a brother or sister he does not talk to? Does he respect his mother?

How he acts on a bad day is information for you. It is his warning, about the way you will learn life lessons in a relationship with him. How he reacts to a problem is how he will teach your future children. When blame and anger are his tools of choice, he teaches your future children that these are their tools of choice.

He is on probation in your life until you see how he reacts on a bad day.

You did not come here into this life to be a mental, emotional or physical punching bag for your partner's inability to handle a bad day.

Excusing bad behaviour

We all find excuses useful. They are a tool to prevent change. When we allow our partner to make excuses, we give him permission to stay the same. It is our nature to want to believe him. But what we are believing is his excuses. We also solidify those excuses, making them acceptable by repeating them to our friends. We say, oh, he is only acting this way because he works hard ..., because he lost his job ..., because he had a bad childhood ..., and so on.

Who has not had bad times or a bad day? We have all had our fair share of tragedy and abuse, but we have not allowed ourselves to turn into abusive people. You will sometimes hear people say how a challenging childhood has created a deep sense of compassion that they would not have had, had they not had those experiences.

By not questioning his excuses we become stuck in negative repeating relationships. We allow him to justify his bad behaviour, when we would never behave like that towards him.

Remember, whatever you accept, you teach your future

children. They observe and replicate. When you have kids, you are training them how they should act in a relationship. You and your partner are role models for what a relationship looks like. Think carefully, do you want him teaching your children what is normal?

Allow the possibility of a partner who treats you better than you treat him. Then you be like him. Your relationship will become one, where you uplift each other to be the best version of yourselves. You will grow together with combined goals of love, peace and forgiveness.

The seventh filtering pattern: Your values

You will not register when he violates your values if you are not consciously aware of your values. When you empathise with his stories, that early attraction can cause you to absorb his values as yours. You then filter his stories based on his values, and you ignore the signs, missing the warning contained within his words.

Your values might say that you do not put down another person; you treat the elderly with respect; you do not abuse your power; you do not attack people and denigrate them. Your values underpin your behaviour. When his stories from the past shock you, that is a sign that he is violating your values.

There are things in our past that we would never reveal because we felt guilt over our actions. In those moments, we violated our values. We would never tell someone about those actions with pride.

But his stories do not shock him, because he did not violate his values. His heroic tales that shock you are not heroic. His values say what he did was okay; your values are telling you through your shocked reaction that what he did was not okay.

Change is not something he is interested in because he has not violated his own values. When you allow a boyfriend into your life who violates your values, you are heading down a dangerous path. When your values are higher than his, he will not respect what you say, especially those things that are important to you, that come from your values. He does not value those things. He will not value you.

His values are telling you what you need to know; they are his warning to you about how your future with him will be.

He does not have his values tattooed on his forehead. His stories of the past are where he reveals his values.

Loyalty contract

Another reason we ignore the signs is that we allow him to treat us in ways that we would never treat him, we remain loyal despite the signs. A key question to ask is, "Would you treat him like that? Would you speak to him the way he speaks to you?"

If he puts you down, refuses to be reasonable, gets angry over minor things, you are not an equal in your relationship. Mutual respect does not exist. Your values do not align, as your values do not allow you to behave like that.

When he inflicts harm or pain and you say to yourself, I would never treat him that way, that is your sign that you are settling for less. Never settle for less. There is a loving partner out there, waiting for you to be single, to show up and meet him.

We use loyalty as a reason to stay. We wait until we are at breaking point before leaving. The loyalty contract is broken by his choices. If he chooses violence, whether it is mental, emotional or physical, he breaks the loyalty contract.

If you would not do it, then do not accept it in a partner. Choose a partner who uplifts your life, someone who inspires you to laugh, who inspires you to be yourself. Value yourself, don't settle.

The eighth filtering pattern: Rushing in

When you meet a guy who ignites that spark, it is easy to start thinking about the future. Thoughts about a possible joyous future creates emotions and your heart follows where your mind goes.

When you envision your happy ending based on time spent with someone you barely know, you stop living in the present, which is where the clues lie as to whether a future is possible. One way to trick your mind into staying in the present is to make a joke out of what your mind is doing. Tell yourself, "settle petal, you hardly know him", or "calm your farm, it's only week two". Find your own fun words to coach your mind into staying in the present.

One possible reason for rushing in is that you tell yourself that you are alone, instead of single. The labels we place on ourselves weigh down on our psyche. If you constantly repeat the mantra, "I am alone", you will feel sad, causing you to search for a partner to remove that sadness.

Calling yourself alone causes you to filter his stories, trade off on his faults and ignore the signs. It is impossible to feel alone if you see yourself as love, but more on that in part two. For now, release the habit of calling yourself alone. Remind yourself you are single, ready to mingle.

Rushing in causes you to fall in love with his good points! The problem is he is not his good points. He is a complex creature, just as you are. In the early days, he is on his best behaviour, as you are.

By rushing in you ignore "what you need to know", and you allow his past to become your future.

The spark

Like a bee is attracted to honey, we attract the lessons we need to learn, as well as who best to learn them from. Look at the spark with scepticism. First look to see which pain in you is in him. What baggage are you carrying that he also has? Baggage is something that pulls us away from love and draws in that which is like itself. It pulls us away from our true core self, which is love.

A simple example. If you have the problem of being chronically late, you may draw in someone who is worse than you. Perhaps this is the universe giving you a gentle nudge, a big stick reminding you that you need to look at why you choose to be chronically late.

Eventually, you may draw in someone who is meticulous about being on time, and who becomes aggressive the second you are late. The sledgehammer effect. How can you learn to be on time without having to draw in a partner to teach you?

Many times, we discard the good guy because we are not attracted to him. We know it would be in our best interests if we were, but we do not feel the spark because we are choosing the sledgehammer way of learning our life lessons.

The spark can lead you to painful lessons. Ask yourself why you have drawn him in. What could he be showing up to teach you? What pattern is being revealed to you? How can you move forward, releasing this pattern to learn it outside a relationship?

Are you chasing the spark and ignoring the good guy? Remember, sparks fade; choose the good guy!

The ninth filtering pattern: Changing him

We believe we can change him. Sometimes we think that because we are different from his past girlfriends, or that because we are quiet and kind, we can change him. However, that is our ego at play. We are not special because we are nice or kind. We cannot turn him into a better person. We cannot release him from his demons.

Our attempt to change him can be a way to avoid standing in our power and setting boundaries. Setting boundaries means knowing your values and why they are important to you. Your values drive your boundaries, allowing you to stand in your power. Your values fuel your actions and help you to know what you will not stand for in a relationship.

If you place your hand in a tiger's mouth, it will bite. It's the same for humans. If he shows you his character, believe him. It is his choice to be this way and you are not going to change him.

The decision to change comes from deep within. It wells up, catapulting us towards transformation. The desire not to be the same, or not to repeat past mistakes, fuels the action required for change. Not all of your niceness, your giving in to his will, your gentle persuasion, or your time convincing him, works.

He might hear you and agree with you and make changes on some small things, but on the big things, the things that really matter, he will not hear you and he will not change.

When we take the focus off our life and place it on his life and fixing him we invite in trouble. We can do this when we are afraid of making changes in our life, and so we try to change him instead of ourselves.

When you feel the urge to change him, ask yourself what are you are avoiding changing in your life. If you could do/be anything, what would that look like? What are your next best steps forward?

You are the owner of your life. You have the power to change your life.

Meditation: To find your values

This exercise is to assist you in unlocking your values, if you are not aware of them, or the values that you would like to align your new self with. Place a notepad and pen beside you for when you finish.

Take some calming breaths. Place your feet on the floor. Feel the energy of Mother Earth flowing up through the soles of your feet. You might notice a colour associated with that energy; if not, it does not matter, just allow that energy to fill and nourish your body.

Now imagine the top of your head is connected to golden strands, those strands reach right up high, becoming finer and more golden.

These strands connect to the wisdom and healing energy of the universe. Now imagine that wisdom and healing energy flowing down the golden strands in and through you, nourishing your entire body. Sit in this energy.

Now imagine yourself in the future. Imagine the highest future you could see for yourself. Let your mind wander. See yourself, happy, joyful, laughing in this imaginary future.

If you could be or do anything, what would it look like? Don't limit yourself; allow yourself to envisage your highest future. What would your dream job be? What does your dream life purpose look like? Picture yourself there. Let yourself dream.

Feel the joy as you allow your heart and soul's purpose to come forward. Sit and watch your amazing self, your potential self.

What qualities does your future-self have? Is your future-self confident, bold, courageous, energetic or strong? What does your future-self stand for?

Now allow the highest qualities of your future-self to absorb into you. Feel them downloading from your future self. Take some relaxed deep breaths whilst these highest qualities flow into and through your current life with grace and ease.

Smile, and gently come back to the room, feeling your toes, the floor, your hands, take a few deep breaths, hear the outside noises, wriggle your shoulders and open your eyes. Take a drink of water.

Write down who your future self is. What does she value in life? What are her qualities? What is her highest purpose?

The five signs and our filtering

Claire

Claire met her boyfriend Blake at a nightclub. He walked in and shook the right people's hands, including the owners. He seemed important and when he paid attention to her, she felt special. They danced all night and the next day went to the local coffee shop. Over coffee he told her, "You shouldn't date me, I have too many issues." His honesty caught her by surprise; she admired him for speaking honestly. She could handle problems. She'd done that all her life.

They started dating and true to her boyfriend's word, she spent the next two years immersed in his problems. He had business partners chasing him for money, the police knocking on her door, and court cases. These dramas were not in her life prior to meeting him. She allowed those things in by discounting the warning he gave her on their first date.

Blake told her what she needed to know. He warned her about whether their relationship was going to bring happiness or hardship. Claire did not have to interpret his words or his vague meaning, or even listen too hard. He told her straight out, "You shouldn't date me, I have too many issues", and she ignored him. She admired him for his honesty and ignored his words. She recreated her past.

Ellen

Ellen met Daniel at a party. They had an instant rapport. He liked yoga, he had a great job and his passion was to make the world a better place. These things ticked boxes in her head.

They went out to dinner the next night. Whilst having their entrées she asked him, "How do you get along with your ex?" He stared silently at her before saying, "She ran off with my best friend and left me in debt and cost me my job."

Ellen was shocked, but listened to his stories and felt empathy for him. That night, Ellen did not sleep well and she had anxiety all the next morning. She spoke to me on the phone the next day. I said to her, I think he's feeding you a sob story, and your body clearly doesn't like something you've heard. Why did his ex run off with his best friend?

The next day she went on another date with Daniel. Once again, he talked about his ex and how she did him wrong. Ellen left the date knowing that Daniel wasn't right for her. She sent him a text message wishing him all the best for the future and said she hoped he would find whom he was searching for.

His reaction to her text confirmed everything. He abused her for leading him on. He told her she was stupid and he was a good catch and that she would be sorry she missed out on him.

He told her what she needed to know on their first and second date. He blamed his ex. He fed her his sob story. Her shock, her restless sleep and anxiety were all signs that she should take notice, his past would show up as her future. She had only wished him well, and his attack on her confirmed not to let him into her life.

Always ask yourself, would you do that? If you wouldn't, then you have a clear message that your values are being violated, and he will never respect you.

Kirsty

One day, Kirsty was with her boyfriend at the beach when they saw a woman sitting out the front of a coffee shop. Her boyfriend said, "Look at that fat loser." Kirsty was shocked and said to him, "Who are you to judge her?"

He agreed that maybe she was right, but Kirsty repeatedly felt his judgment on her life and her friends' lives. He never changed and she ignored the signs by thinking she could be the one to change him.

Gauge his promises to change by his actions. Children do not listen to your words; they listen to your actions. When you were a child, how many times did you tune out when your mother or father spoke? Maybe it was when they confiscated your phone or threw your favourite toy in the bin that you paid attention. The same is true with your partner. If you are hearing promises to change and seeing nothing, then that is your cue to take action and get going out the door.

The job interview

The second and third dates are the job interview. The position as your boyfriend is open. You have already filtered out anyone you are not interested in and anyone who is not suitable. The second and third dates are when the job interview cranks up.

You have your list ready. You will not stand for commitment

phobias, carelessness with money, jealousy, blame, anger, violence, etc. Thinking of the early dates as a job interview can shift your perspective. As the interviewer, you have all the power to choose the best candidate, not just for your future, but your future children.

Consider what kind of role model will he be to your future children? Is he equivalent to or better than the role models you have had in your life? Who are your role models and how did they shape you into who you are? Who do you consider to be your current role models? Who inspires you and what about them inspires you?

Looks and charm fade, but a genuine person will always shine.

Moving on

Sometimes boyfriends or partners come into our life to move us to the next level, revealing old baggage that has been controlling us. He comes in with a rush of energy, everything changes, and then the universe makes its move and he is gone. It turns out he was part of a bigger picture. He needed to come in and he needed to leave. His leaving was the catalyst for us to change.

Our best learning can occur after a breakup, which is why taking some time out to heal, to see an alternative therapist, or to journal your thoughts can bring the insight needed to uncover the beliefs hiding behind your life patterns.

Where is the universe asking you to move, grow and change? The universe is operating in your favour. Do not be disappointed because he has gone. That disappointment can be the stepping stone, the fuel to change to meet a greater love and step up to a greater life.

Now is the time to create a new relationship in alignment with your values, in alignment with the person you have always wanted to be.

Filtering and the signs: Online dating

In the online world, anyone can be anybody. Profile pictures can be stolen. They can be years out of date. Profiles can be fictitious. Use the signs and your knowledge of the filtering patterns to guide your questions and to review his photos and words. Look for his values within his words and pictures.

Exclude all profile names that refer to anything sexual or quick, such as "erotic4you", or "goodforonenight". The dating app is there to protect you. Stay within it and follow its safety guidelines.

We have been in the digital age long enough now to have clear photos. If he has sunglasses or a hat on in every photo ask why is trying to disguise himself. The eyes are windows to the soul. Make sure you can see him clearly.

Pictures of him with lots of girls or drinking alcohol – ask yourself, would you do that? If he is posing next to his expensive car and in exotic overseas locations, ask yourself why he needs to show off his financial status. What is he lacking in his personality that he needs to give you a list of assets to entice you into swiping yes? Check in, are you following your ticked boxes list and ignoring the signs?

If he is messaging sexual innuendos, avoid him. Your intuition is your guide. If you get the feeling something is off, then acknowledge your gut instinct and do not proceed. Ensure you are not filtering his message by rushing in.

If you wish to proceed and want to speak with him, let him give you his number and call him with your number set to private. During the phone conversation, ask him about his likes and dislikes. Ask him about his past. What would his ex say was his worst aspect? Let the conversation unfold and you will hear what you need to know. Hear the signs. You are the prize, not him.

If you are falling in love without ever meeting, then you have been talking online for too long. It is not the real world and everything exchanged in messages can be a lie. Ask yourself is he seducing you with his stories? Does he have a profile on other social media platforms where you can verify who he is? Do you know anyone who knows him? The world is actually very small, so ask around.

Do not friend him on your other social media platforms. Make sure you have them locked down to private so he cannot find you, and if he does find you, why is he looking? What are his motives? This is your clue to avoid him as he is acting obsessively. Femicide is a stark reality that women can't ignore. Around one woman a week is killed by a current or an ex-partner in Australia. Sadly this is replicated around the world

Do not put your birth year in your social media usernames or email address. In some countries, a person only needs your birthdate and your mother's maiden name to steal your identity.

Tell him straight early on that you are only interested in a relationship and you are not interested in a fling. Put this in bold in your profile. If he goes away, then he was not the right person for you; there is someone better out there.

Are there constant roadblocks preventing you from meeting? Could he be hiding which country he is in? If so, you are potentially chatting with a catfish. A catfish is someone sitting in a room, chatting to multiple females, with one goal: to extract money from you. Write in your profile: no international connections. Choose a dating app where you can lock the area down to your country or your state, to help eliminate catfishing.

If you are on a dating app that you cannot lock down to exclude international connections, what you may see from these international connections is that he does not read your profile. Write in your profile something significant like "I am writing a book", and you will see that he makes no mention of it in his first contact. He is sending his standard catfishing message out hoping to hook you in. Educate yourself. Look into the extensive range of books and interviews warning you about the dangers of catfishing.

If you do decide to meet up, make sure it is in a public place during daylight hours. Send his details to a friend or family member. Have a friend phone to check on you. Ask your family members to follow you via an app or phone-tracking to check on your whereabouts.

If you are contented in your life and you feel a greater life is calling you, then online dating may not be for you. Think about joining a meet-up or an artist group where you can expand your mind in your area of interest and meet people with similar interests. Life exists in the real world; show up and live yours there, as much as you can.

Prayer to the universe: Show me the truth that I may see the person before me more clearly.

Nikki

Nikki, 19, was chatting with a guy aged 22 on an online dating site. In his profile, he had pictures of himself on holiday overseas, next to his motorbike and high-end car. He matched with her ticked boxes list – financially secure. She asked him, "What would your ex-girlfriend say was your worst habit?" He said, "I can't think of anything." She rephrased the question and he said he still couldn't come up with anything. Nikki knew she was hearing a sign. His warning – not being able to think of anything – was telling her what she needed to know. Something's not right with this guy.

He told her that he followed the stock market every morning and he got up early to collect data from the overnight markets. She thought this was strange, as boys around her age didn't normally go to such effort with their finances.

They met in the city for dinner. The busy traffic delayed her 30 minutes. She laughed to herself, thinking it was most likely a sign that she was wasting her time. She walked up to the restaurant and saw a man standing outside the door. He looked over 40; he couldn't be her date. She looked around. No one else was in sight. She looked at him again. He was smiling at her. "Oh God, it's him!"

She was not interested and instead of speaking up and saying goodnight, she decided to be polite and have dinner with him. They sat inside a booth with nowhere to look but at each other. He told her about a condominium that his ex-girlfriend had lived in, and that she too could live there one day. She was shocked; was he propositioning her? When she moved her hand onto the table, he placed his hand gently on top of hers and stared smilingly into her eyes. She couldn't whip her hands off the table quick enough. She spent the rest of the dinner with her hands in her lap.

The coffee arrived and he asked, "What do you think of me?" She replied that she did not think they had a connection, instead of telling him the truth – that she was not interested. He pursued her over the next few days, until eventually, she messaged him saying she was not interested. Nikki had many signs along the way and seeing him outside the restaurant should have been her cue to walk away.

We are not under any obligation to be compliant, especially when he has broken the basic law of online dating – at least resemble your profile picture. We need to understand that being polite includes saying no. We are not under any obligation to say yes to anyone. We end up wasting their time and our time by hiding the truth in the misguided belief that saying no isn't polite.

Nikki allowed ticking boxes to guide her actions. She filed his story as strange when he told her he was up early looking at the stock market. His behaviour at the restaurant confirmed that she had her warning. When he doesn't share, or he can't think of anything negative his ex would say, then he is sharing plenty and he is telling you what you need to know – not to pursue anything further with him.

Highlights

- Discern how you are filtering his message.
- Listen out for the truth serum.
- Has he revealed that his ex has anxiety or depression now? Do not ignore the signs; you might just end up the same as her.
- You are single, not alone.
- View the spark as your attraction to lessons. Can you learn these lessons elsewhere in a positive way, through your career, your hobbies?
- Remember, it is a job interview and the most important position is open: your boyfriend.
- Are you allowing him to justify his bad behaviour?
- Are you focusing on changing him as an excuse not to make changes in your own life?
- Nobody can talk you into change. It is a deep desire to live differently than you did in your past.
- Know your values. If his values are lower than yours are, he will always be moving you down to his.
- Are you continuously choosing guys who have lower values than yours? If so, what is driving your attraction to them?
- If he is not taking responsibility for his behaviour, change is not on his radar.
- Does he treat you in ways that you would never treat him? Remember, if you have children with him, they learn from him. Is he worthy to be the father of your children?

- Online dating requires additional caution; you do not know him, and you may not know anyone who does know him. If he's asking for money, potentially, you are being catfished. Don't fall in love with him before meeting him in the real world.
- Always remember the good does not outweigh the bad.
- You deserve better. You are worthy of better.

The nine filtering patterns summary

Ticking boxes

- Beware when you find yourself ticking boxes. You have stopped paying attention to his warning.

Seduced by his stories

- Is he charming you with his stories? Is he painting himself as the victim, the hero, the joker?

Honesty

- Are you admiring him for his honesty? Has he told you stories of violence that you are ignoring because you are focusing on the fact that he is being honest?

The past

- Are you filing his stories as one-off past events? Are you ignoring their message?

- Is he telling you how he has grown and learnt from the past?

His ex's fault

- Has he sucked you into his sob story? Has he painted his ex as a psycho, out-of-control bitch? Is he taking no responsibility for the past?

- Does he blame his ex? Is he telling you she was the cause of his negative behaviour? Be aware that his past may show up as your future. You may end up like her.

Good day

- You know how he reacts on a good day; that's why you've gone on a second date!
- You need to know how he reacts on a bad day. He is on probation until you know how he handles a bad day.

Your values

- Are you filtering his stories based on his values? Have his stories shocked you? Do you know your values? Is he hooking you into his lesser values?

Rushing in

- Are you falling in love too quickly? Have you fallen in love with his good points and ignored his bad points? Are you reminding yourself you are single, not alone?
- Look at the spark with scepticism. First look to see which pain in you is in him.

Changing him

- Beware on those early dates when you filter his story by deciding what you can change in him.

❧ Reflections ❧

If you are in a relationship or about to enter one, do you carry the following beliefs?

1. Do you believe you can change him?

If yes, does anyone have a right to change you? Do you have the right to change anyone else? Each person, no matter what path they are on, has the right to live that path. If you have done what is ethically responsible to help another, then your focus needs to be on your life and the lives of your children, if you have them.

2. Do you believe that your partner will change because you are kind and gentle?

When we are brought up to be the peacemaker, we can find ourselves living in a state of compromise, not fully looking after ourselves or our children, constantly doing things to make someone else happy. It is not our path to be a doormat for our boyfriend to use and abuse. Your soul is beautiful and you deserve a partner who uplifts your life to joy, just as you do so for him.

After-date questions:

Are you basing his character only on his good points, instead of who he is telling you he is?

Are you ignoring the signs because you are ticking the boxes?

Does he blame his ex?

Does his ex have depression, anxiety or other symptoms now?

Does he justify his bad behaviour?

How does he handle stressful situations?

Are you valuing his honesty and ignoring his message?

Are you rushing in?

CHAPTER 3

HISTORY

"What you resist persists."
— Carl Jung

Dating the family

We are each born into a family situation which brings us the opportunity to learn and grow our soul. This is cold comfort for those who have experienced damaging childhoods, especially when, as adults, you realise you have replicated those childhoods.

We date our perception of the negative and positive aspects of our father, mother, brother, sister, or grandparents' personality. We have learnt that these negative and positive aspects are normal; they feel familiar even if they are painful and so we repeat our familiar family patterns unconsciously.

Dating our family's positive aspects is not a problem as it does not cause us pain. We often believe that by escaping a traumatic childhood we are free to live the life that we never had. But this freedom is a myth, because those negative family aspects follow us into our relationships and into our working life.

If one parent was controlling, aggressive or put you down, chances are you will bring in partners who do the same, and if not partners, it will be friends, co-workers and bosses. This is our soul's growth in this lifetime; releasing the grudges, the resentments, the hurt; standing in our power and finding our way back to love.

When we "date" our family's negative traits, these are our own personal perceptions. If we have siblings, even if close in age, they will all have different perceptions and wounds from their childhood. When you see negative family traits reappearing in your life, you begin to realise the power those traits have over you.

We would not spend as much time in destructive relationships if we realised we are there for the "learning effect". Usually, the fact that we are reliving learnt childhood patterns goes unseen by us. We stay in relationships, thinking we are doing the right thing by persevering with our partners.

Each new relationship gives us the opportunity to work through and overcome destructive childhood patterns, to release the control those patterns have over us.

I have dated all aspects of my parents' and siblings' positive and negative traits. With each partner, I recognised which parent or sibling I was bringing in. It was only when I moved into awareness of my values and understood the five signs and nine filtering patterns, that I began to break this pattern.

When meeting someone new, ask yourself where his past is colliding with your patterns.

Our partners

What we dislike about our family's personalities we can attract in our boyfriends/partners/husband. Our boyfriends will have a ramped-up version of our siblings' and parents' personality aspects. Holding on to anger and resentment towards your family draws those personalities into your life. These same personalities can appear in your working life as co-workers and bosses. Becoming aware is the start of breaking the pattern.

Ask yourself, "Who do I resent? Who can I not forgive? What can I not forgive? Who harmed me and when? What happened?" These are clues to the personalities you can subconsciously draw in.

Sometimes we need to journal about our past to realise the patterns that we have been repeating. There is amazing power in writing your story. Often, until we get it down on paper, we do not realise what we've been recreating. Just start writing. Don't think you need to write an epic novel; the main point is to keep the pen moving to allow your story to unfold.

Release blaming your parents. If your parents could have done better, they would have. One day you may be a parent and your children will probably have complaints about you. At any moment, you can strive to do better, so let the past be the past and be the change you want to see in others, otherwise you will draw in partners matching with those negative aspects you carry.

You are not the disempowered child anymore.

The narcissist

We often hear the term "narcissist", perhaps in movies or on TV. For many of us, this has created the belief that narcissism means to overly love yourself, this meaning being drawn from the Greek mythological story, where Narcissus fell in love with his own reflection. But the modern use of the term narcissist has evolved from Freudian psychiatry.

The narcissistic personality details presented here are based on my life experience and observations, they are not presented as a medical diagnosis nor to diagnose or treat anyone.

In its worst embodiment, this personality type can bring you to the brink of destruction and despair. This personality type can undermine your self-esteem and cause you to question your relevance in this world.

One way you can think of narcissism is that you are having a relationship with a spoilt child who lives in an adult's body, and the personality of the spoilt child controls his mind and actions. I have found the narcissist personality trait to be so prevalent in our modern world that it is something that everyone should be aware of as it can lead to coercive control.[1]

No one is immune to this personality trait. No gender is immune to this personality trait. The narcissist in your past

---

[1] Coercive Control examples: isolating you from family & friends, manipulation, controlling your access to money, controlling what you eat & wear, monitoring your activity/location, restricting freedom, put-downs, jealousy & possessiveness, threats & intimidation.

or present can be a parent, a grandparent, a sibling, a friend or a co-worker.

A narcissist at their worst is absorbed in how great they are. Paranoia, jealousy, secrecy and a lack of empathy are typical. No one's needs are more important than theirs.

Dating the narcissist

Things move fast when you date a narcissist. One minute you are single, the next you are entwined in his web of mental games. Some favourites are: "I want you, but I don't want you", "Let me tell you your faults", or he can ignore you for days because you have "hurt him". He has a huge list of offences, and at any random point in time, he can accuse you of one of them.

I have found a narcissist is insecure and afraid on the inside and has a deep need to make you feel as bad as he does. On the outside, he can be confident and highly intelligent. He can be charming and win your friends over with his charisma and outgoing personality. Shy versions exist also, sitting alone at your family functions, separating you from family and friends.

He may not get along with his own family, and he may put them down. Your family is not important to him and having them close to you does not suit him. He will do what he can to alienate you from them and create a distance between you. He cannot have you obtaining love and support from anyone outside of him. If you have an external support system, you will eventually grow strong, stand up to him and leave him.

He loves listing your faults, but then will refer to you as his princess, or that you should be treated like one. You will wonder why he wants to date you, when all he can see are faults within you. He needs to put you down. He cannot have you receiving greater applause than him or outshining him.

He needs you to be dependent upon him, mentally and emotionally, otherwise he cannot play with you, knocking you off your happy perch when he wants to. You can be happy, when it suits him.

A common attack of his will be to tear you (or your future children) down, out of nowhere. A sudden attack over nothing is his weapon of choice. He may then follow this up with the silent treatment, which can last for days. He loves having you wonder what you have done wrong.

Mental and emotional torture is his delight, and depending on the degree of narcissism, he will intersperse this with periods of physical or sexual abuse.

He will tell you it is your fault he is angry. You caused him to be angry by ... looking out the window, by looking at someone on the street, by wearing lipstick, for wearing a push-up bra. The more ridiculous his accusation, the more he seems to get off on it. You are his toy. Blame is his missile and you are his target.

You will notice his behaviour is childlike. He throws a tantrum when he does not get his way. Disagreeing with him will set him off. He loves to attack for the smallest of reasons. You are his toy. You are not his equal in the relationship.

When you need a partner to provide you with love, with your reason for living, with your purpose, you are in the danger zone for attracting a narcissist.

The narcissist list

When you say something he doesn't like, what is his reaction? Is it negative, aggressive, attacking? Does he put you down? Does he focus on your faults? Ask yourself, "Would I do that? Would I react that way?" Remember, change is not on a narcissist's radar.

This list is based on my observations and life experience. This is not an exhaustive list.

- He acts like a child.
- He is easily aggravated.
- He lacks empathy.
- He gets into a bad mood over the smallest issue.
- He gets upset when he doesn't get his way.
- He analyses every small detail you tell him.
- He does not respond to logic.
- He does not connect with his family or he does not like his family.
- He does not like to hear the word no.
- He does not listen to what you say.
- He tries to separate you from your family.
- He makes up stories in his head and then attacks you with those stories.
- He tears you down.
- He throws back in your face the personal details you have shared with him.
- He has no tolerance for being late.

- He has no tolerance, full stop.
- He is anxious, nervous and agitated about his time schedule.
- He is happy one minute, psychotic and angry the next.
- He tells you there is nothing wrong with him; it is you!
- He asks you to stop wearing makeup.
- He tells you your clothes are too revealing.
- He tells you, you are a princess, that everyone should treat you like one.
- He tells you, you are hot and sexy in regular conversation.
- He feeds you chocolate and foods that aggravate your skin or health. Then criticises you.
- He blames his ex-girlfriend or ex-wife.
- He tells you all women are whores (including his sisters).
- He tells you his ex was psycho, she has anxiety or she is an alcoholic, etc.
- A few weeks into meeting him, he tells you not to get fat.
- He never has his own money to take you out, but he has plenty of money to go out with his mates.

Important:

Consult your doctor, psychologist, qualified health care practitioner for help in dealing with narcissistic partners, friends, co-workers or family members and other antisocial personality disorders such as sociopaths, etc.

A narcissist does not seek to empower you, or to empower others; tearing you down is your clue to who he is.

HISTORY

Emily

Emily met her new boyfriend, Michael, one Sunday afternoon for coffee. They had been dating for two weeks. After ordering their coffee, Emily went to the cakes display to choose a dessert. She then walked back to the table, smiling, excited with her selection. "I've ordered the French vanilla slice!" Michael didn't respond. She said it again a bit louder, smiling at the thought of the slice melting in her mouth, and still Michael said nothing. She asked, "Is something the matter?" He took a deep breath, looked out the window and did not respond.

Their coffee and cake date turned into a disaster. He could barely crack a smile and would only speak when necessary. The whole way back to their cars, Emily pleaded with him to let her know what was wrong. He had her caught in his web.

A narcissist's greatest joy is to have you wonder how you have offended him. As soon as his childish behaviour appears, you have your signal to get out fast.

Samantha

Samantha's partner moved in with her after her flatmate moved out. From the moment he moved in, he took ownership over the apartment. He took it upon himself to repaint the lounge room and have the carpet steam-cleaned. Any marks or dirt were something she had done to offend him.

One day he called her to the kitchen to ask when she had last washed the floor. The next day it was the fridge: how long was that juice in there, how long was she going to leave it there? She only knew how to defend herself. Soon she found herself defending and explaining herself constantly.

The narcissist will turn his obsessions into offences committed by you against him. Each thing you do or don't do is a crime in his eyes. Defending yourself is playing into his hands. Refusing to drop down to his level of anger disorientates him as his game is to provoke you.

Amanda

One day Amanda made beef burgundy. She was so proud of herself. It was her first attempt at making something healthy without using any pre-packaged ingredients.

She set the table with a new cloth and decorated it with flowers she had bought. Her partner took one gulp and spat it out on her clean tablecloth. "What's that?! Are you trying to poison me?" He stood up, picked up his plate, threw it at the bin and walked out.

Amanda spent years explaining herself, crying, not realising she was the toy in his game.

Brittany

Brittany invited her new boyfriend over to meet her parents on Christmas Eve. All seemed well, but Brittany's new boyfriend suddenly stopped talking to her late that evening. Days went by and the boyfriend continued his mood.

After a few days, he explained that Brittany reminded him of his ex-girlfriend after seeing her in a similar dress on Christmas Eve, which put him in a confused state as to whether he wanted to date her or not. Brittany asked, "But why did you have to stop talking to me on Christmas Eve, when we were having a special night with my mum and dad? You could have just told me." He had no response to logic.

After six months together, Brittany's boyfriend started making demands. The first one was that she stop wearing lipstick. A few weeks later, it was eyeliner and mascara. He did not want her wearing makeup when she went shopping. Sometime later, he found fault with her clothes. Why did she have to dress up when she went shopping? After that, he decided her tops were too revealing. He quizzed her constantly on what she was doing and where she was going and why was she wearing so much makeup.

He hacked into her email and deleted her Snapchat account. He smashed her laptop against the wall when he found photos of her ex-boyfriend on it. He questioned why she needed to be on social media. She deleted her accounts to keep the peace, but he didn't delete his.

The breakthrough for Brittany was to regroup with her family. They started going to the gym together, to the movies and out for dinner. Bit by bit, Brittany's confidence came back. Her parents booked appointments for her with psychologists and therapists who, after a year, guided Brittany back to her old "new" self.

Breaking free – Sarah's story

Sarah had been in a relationship with a narcissist. Realising she needed to get out, she started rebuilding her self-esteem through going to the gym and seeing a professional psychologist, which is where this story starts.

Sarah was walking into the shopping centre with her

boyfriend. A gust of wind blew and her long fringe became tangled. She opened her bag and took out her comb. Her boyfriend grabbed the comb and threw it back into the parking lot, whilst asking, "Who are you fixing your hair for?"

Sarah said, "Not for you, that's for sure." She turned and walked back to her car, leaving him standing there.

Another time they were at a restaurant. After a pleasant evening, the bill came. Sarah waited for her boyfriend to pay as she was determined not to pay this time. He would always have an excuse as to why he couldn't pay: he left his wallet at home, or he didn't work much that week. But he constantly wore the latest designer clothing and had the newest mobile phone on the market.

"What are you waiting for, pay the bill, bitch!"

"I don't think so ... and I'm not paying the bill ever again!" She picked up her handbag and walked out, never to see him again.

Do not go back

The narcissist will promise to be better and stop his controlling behaviour. You may find him to be true to his word for three or four weeks and life will be blissful for that time, when he loves you and treats you as the love of his life. However, his willpower to change does not last, nor does he want to change, as he does not believe that he has a problem.

Even if the relationship does not end badly, by blocking him you are affirming that you are ready to move on. You affirm to the universe: "Next! I'm ready for someone better." Know that your "next" has been waiting for you to be single. He has been waiting for you to choose a higher life. A life where you choose love, joy and happiness.

Seek professional help to extricate yourself from a narcissist. Realise the signs early to remove yourself from his web.

A greater love has been calling you, a love where you are respected, valued and appreciated for who you are.

Gaslighting

Gaslighting is a term made famous by the movie of the same name. In the movie, the gaslights dim then brighten. However, the husband tells his wife that it is all in her imagination.

Gaslighting can be used as a form of control, and its aim is to have you living in a state of constant confusion. Causing you to lose confidence in yourself as you constantly second guess your memories and perceptions of things.

The gaslighter likes to revise history and take advantage of any memory lapses you might have. They like to make themselves out as the victim. The gaslighter in your past might have been a parent, a grandparent or a sibling. Be aware that gaslighting is a tactic that narcissists can use on you.

Love

Love may be easier to understand by defining what it is not. Love is not fear. Love is not jealousy. Love does not seek to control or take power over another. Sometimes we confuse love with security and choose partners based on fear. Him saying, "I love you and that is why I hit you" is not love.

Our natural state is to be love. We are the ones who feel bad when we hate. A negative opinion we hold about someone makes us feel bad and takes our peace away. Love is freedom. Love inspires creativity. Harmony, bliss and abundance are the result of love. What love touches, it grows. Love is the gateway to joy.

We cannot run from ourselves. If you are blocking love and are unable to find inspiration in your life, then you will try to extract that love and inspiration from your partner. You will need his praise, his comfort, his love, his goals, to fuel your life. Your partner is not here to fill in the parts of you that you think are missing.

Building a life through what inspires you is one pathway forward to find the joy living within you. This allows you to draw in boyfriends/partners/husbands who resonate with that same joy.

Meditation: Return to love exercise

Lift your vibration and know yourself as love. We attract in that which we are. Use this exercise to lift you to a higher state before you go out or off to work.

Think of a time when you truly felt loved and at peace. It may have been at a beach on sunset, a time when you were on holidays. It might be spending time with a pet, or gazing at a baby.

Close your eyes. Take a deep breath and relax. Go back to your experience, whether it's with your pet, or it's a sunset or whatever. Just imagine you are there now.

See, sense, feel the air around you. Is it a sunny day? Are you inside or outside? Can you feel the warmth of the sun or a breeze? What are you wearing? What sounds do you hear? Do you hear the sounds of birds or water? If it's your pet you're imagining, what sounds does it make? Are you holding it? Is it snuggling in next to you? Is there a fragrance in the air? Feel the joy building inside. Breathe gently and relax into the experience. Enjoy this space for a few minutes then gently open your eyes, have a drink of water.

This is how you return to love. When we move away from love, we feel pain. When we feel love, we feel great. It is that simple. To stay out of pain, love someone or something, and you will return to your natural state, which is love.

Empower yourself

We are told forgiveness will help release us from the past, but often forgiveness is easier said than done. Often we have not received an apology for the things that have truly hurt us, or if we did receive one, it has not satisfied us. The apology did not bring closure because it was not said how we wanted to hear it, or we felt the apology was not genuine, and so forgiveness eludes us.

Most people these days understand that forgiveness does not mean condoning behaviour or allowing it to happen again. A new way to think of forgiveness is, "I release myself from the belief that you ever hurt me."

If we choose to be the victim, we allow pain and illness into our lives as a way of justifying how they hurt us, and justifying our blame towards them. Choosing the mindset that "I am impervious to what you did" releases you. The act we felt disempowered from no longer exists.

With this mindset, you no longer allow your mental and emotional energy to leak out by giving them any of your valuable mind or emotional space. Ask yourself, why would you want them in your mind?

Also, if they are in your mind, they are in your body.

That is enough reason to never to want to hold pain about anyone.

Affirmation: I release that you ever hurt me. I am and I always will be, impervious to you.

Forgiveness exercise

This is a powerful exercise that you can do anytime and many times over.

Find a quiet area where you won't be disturbed for 5 minutes, preferably seated or sitting on the floor. Place your hands up to form an open circle – as if you are holding an invisible balloon. Imagine between your hands is a circle of gold light. Ask you guide, angel or higher self to assist you.

Imagine the person you are having trouble forgiving is now within your circle. You can imagine them as a stick figure or just have a sense that is them within your circle.

Then imagine a gold cord between your heart and theirs.

Now imagine you have a gold pair of scissors, and as you say the words, you are going to cut the cord, "I do not know why you did what you did, I do not know why you said what you said ..."

"... but I forgive you and release you in my love."

Repeat these words, and if you can, send love from your heart to theirs.

(Do not worry if your imaginary scissors don't appear to cut the cord; just know that it has cut it all the way through.)

Keep saying the words ...

Say the words "I do not know why you did what you did, I do not know why you said what you said ..."

"... but I forgive you and release you in my love."

Continue until you feel the person leave the gold circle, or until you intuitively feel your hands come down, usually within five or so minutes.

Thank your angel, guide or higher self, and go about your day.

You can do this exercise on more than one person at once, that is, you can put more people in the circle, and you can do the forgiveness exercise as many times as you feel you need to forgive them.

Self-forgiveness

You can also do this exercise for self-forgiveness by placing yourself in the gold circle and connecting the gold cord. You can imagine a label with an issue, for example, resentment.

The words would change to the below, whilst you use your gold scissors to cut the cord:

"I do not know why I did what I did ... I do not know why I said what I said ... but I forgive myself for my (resentment) ... and I release the (resentment) in my love." (We do not release ourselves.)

Note:
If you are feeling uplifted after completing this chapter, you may wish to skip the highlights and tasks at this point and move to the end of part one, and return to the highlights and tasks if and when it feels right to you.

Highlights

- We date our family.

- Holding on to anger and resentment towards your family draws those same personalities into your life, whether through relationships, co-workers or bosses.

- Loving yourself and knowing what you value is crucial to avoid inviting a narcissist into your life.

- A narcissist's biggest triumph is to attack you and tell you, you have offended him for something you have no clue about.

- The narcissist behaves like a child when he does not get his way. This is a clue to his true personality.

- You grew up long ago and left the defiant child behind. You don't need a child as a boyfriend.

- Would you behave this way? Allow in a partner who matches with your values.

- You are your children's protector. Do not let anyone into your life who does not uplift your children's mental and emotional state.

- Seek out a partner who uplifts you, who encourages you in your goals, someone who is proud of you.

- A weak person attacks and bullies.

- You are a strong, magnificent person, who is not a victim, but is victorious.

- You now stand in your power as the glorious person you are.

- Empower yourself through courses, therapy,

meditation, mindfulness, yoga and exercise; there are many paths to healing – find the right one for you.

- Seek help: counsellors, doctors, psychologists, trained professionals.

Know that you gain wisdom each day to know who you are and what you value. Know that you can enter into a new relationship without repeating the past. You can bring in a partner who loves and uplifts you, who respects you and who is proud of you.

I know you can because I believe in you.

HISTORY

❧ Reflections ❧

Dating questions (casually weave into your conversation)

Q: Do you think that personal growth is important?
You want to know whether he has any interest in change.

Q: What are your career aspirations?
You want to know if he has grandiose, inflated opinions of himself, that is, he tells you he wants to be a movie star, but isn't even taking acting lessons, etc.

Q: Are you looking for a relationship? Do you want a girlfriend or a long-term partner?
If he tells you he does not want a serious relationship, believe him! A guy does not say what he does not believe. You cannot change him. Do not think that you will be the one who will make him commit.

Q: How did your last relationship break up? What's your favourite thing to do when out with the boys?
You want to know if there has been violence in his life. How does he treat women when out with the boys?

Q: How well do you get along with your brothers and sisters? Is there anyone in your family you do not speak with and why?
Perhaps he avoids dealing with problems and shuts people out. Why doesn't he speak with his family? Watch out for the narcissist who distances himself from his siblings.

Q: How do you get along with your boss and your co-workers? What frustrates you about your job? How often do you change your job?
These questions let you know how he problem-solves. Does he walk away from conflict with bosses and co-workers? It gives you an insight into how he will treat situations when the going gets tough in a relationship with him.

End of relationship pick-me-ups!

When I first started writing this book, I began here. I wanted something uplifting and positive and a bit fun to remind me why my relationship ending was perfect for my life.

Use these sayings to motivate you, to inspire you. Find the ones that resonate with you. Enjoy!

He broke up with me

He broke up with me. Great! Now I'm free to meet my true love.

He broke up with me. Great! Now I'm available to meet the love of my life.

He broke up with me. Great! Now I'm free from his pulling and pushing. ("I want you, but I don't want you.")

He broke up with me. Great! I'm the lucky one to be rid of him.

He broke up with me. Great! I'm now available to meet that sweet, loving guy who's just been waiting to hear I'm single.

He broke up with me. Great! I'm now available, universe!

He broke up with me. Great! I dodged a bullet.

He broke up with me. Great! I'm free to meet a loving life partner and soulmate.

He broke up with me. Great! I knew I'd settled for less.

He broke up with me. Great! Now the arguments are over.

He broke up with me. Great! I'm manifesting a new future.

He broke up with me. Great! I can see clearly now (the blinkers are gone).

He broke up with me. Great! The universe has been waiting to match me with a loving, respectful guy.

He chose to ...

He chose to run off; he doesn't get to choose to run back.

He chose to run away; I choose to prosper.

He chose anger; I choose my life purpose.

He chose to blame; I choose to shine.

He chose to lie; I choose to thrive.

The girlfriend wisdom

We're glad he's gone! He was bringing you down.

We're glad he's gone! It's time for someone better.

We're glad he's gone! You can put yourself first.

We're glad he's gone! You deserve bliss.

We're glad he's gone; there is a greater love waiting for you.

Your wisdom

Good, he's gone – I can do better.

Good, he's gone – my life is looking better already!

Good, he's gone – I knew I settled for less.

Good, he's gone – I've learnt I do not have to go through that ever again.

Good, he's gone – I'm moving forward and not looking back.

Good, he's gone – I am free to achieve my dreams.

Good, he's gone – I made him my world, now I'm making me my world.

Good, he's gone – I'm free to manifest a loving guy.

Good, he's gone – there is a gorgeous, stable, loving guy out there who is rapt to hear I am single.

Words of wisdom from your soulmate/life partner's soul to yours

Keep the faith. I am here, I am waiting for us to meet.

Keep the faith. I'm looking forward to meeting you.

Keep the faith. Divine timing is organising our meeting.

Keep the faith. I can't wait to meet you!

Wisdom from the elders

Rejoice – you are free to joyously create your future now.

Rejoice – your future self has been waiting for you.

Rejoice – your future starts now.

Rejoice – you were born to shine and bring joy to yourself and others.

Wisdom from the universe

We are delighted we can bring forward a loving life partner and soulmate.

We are delighted you can now shine in your own right.

We are delighted you can now stand in your creative power.

We are delighted to help you bring forward your best life.

We are delighted to help show you there is a higher love.

End of Part 1

By asking empowering questions, solutions evolve that would not be available had you asked a disempowering question.

Move forward knowing that you are a glorious being, fuelled by love, empowered by your values, strengthened by your place on this earth, and enlightened through the wisdom of the past.

PART TWO

CHAPTER 4

TRANSFORMATION

"You have power over your mind, not outside events. Realise this, and you will find strength."
— Marcus Aurelius, *Meditations*

In part two of this book, we focus on our inner transformation. We often think "I just need to find the right guy", but the right guy eludes us because we look at life through tainted glasses, those glasses being our beliefs, attitudes and behaviours, which hide the right guy from us.

We draw in boyfriends, partners, friends and work colleagues who match our energetic or vibrational state. People whom we find difficult match with our lowest state. Those whom we find loving, caring and just great people to be around match with our highest state, our higher level of consciousness, that part of us which resonates with love.

Einstein said, "No problem can be solved from the same level of consciousness that created it." It is new ideas created through uplifted thoughts that lead to outcomes that could never be envisaged if we stayed trapped in the mindset of the problem. We now shift ourselves from the mindset of the problem – dating the past – to creating our new future, drawing in life partners/boyfriends/soulmates based on love, joy and happiness.

In these next chapters you will learn to gently evolve and uplift your consciousness, allowing you to release the hold the past has had over you. At the bottom of each section you will find either a positive statement or a positive affirmation to help uplift you to your new dominant vibration, which is love.

This then leads you into part three, where we work with the energy of manifestation to create the relationship your heart has been yearning for.

Your first steps

A major part of your inner transformation is transforming your outer world. Whilst reading this chapter, focus on cleaning up, throwing out, painting and transforming your bedroom. Whether you repaint walls, furniture, or declutter, less is more.

Transform your bedroom into a haven that supports the new you. Change is easier when you use your outer environment to support your inner transformation.

Monica

Monica, 23, spent years repeating the past, dating guys without goals, and with dependency issues. Her first step to freedom after each breakup was to remodel her room, but her biggest transformation came after building a closet. Her clothes previously hung on a clothes rack in her room as her closet was too small.

Building a closet seemed like an insignificant change, but as she sat in her room after it was completed, with her clothes neatly put away, she no longer felt like a child. Her room now felt like an adult's room. Her room reflected the inner state she was trying to reflect in her outer world.

From that point onwards, she started listening to self-help audio books, something she never did before. Within weeks, she attracted in a partner who had a career, a sense of where he was going and, more importantly, he respected her for who she was, a magnificent being, a kind human, a loving child of the universe.

Learning through pain

Many of us have the belief that we need to learn through pain, learning the hard way. This may have occurred due to the experiences we had in our childhood and our school years. This pattern does not serve us; it just adds time to our ultimate goal of breaking the habit of dating our past.

Declare to the universe that you wish to learn through grace and ease. Make the decision and create it as a mantra. This decision and affirmation will gently release you from the pattern of creating life events and drawing in partners who teach you through pain.

This doesn't mean that painful events won't happen. It just means that you will start to reduce the time you stay stuck in painful events. You will realise the lesson early and take steps to move forward more quickly.

I now choose to learn with grace and ease. I release myself from learning through hardship and pain. I uplift my life to love.

What you hate in another

The people we attract into our lives mirror our inner self. Something in them is also in us. Those who challenge us show us where we have moved away from love. Each belief which moves us away from love can be seen mirrored in our relationships, whether in romantic relationships, work relationships, our friendship groups or relatives.

Those people who resonate with our loving self do not bother us. Those who resonate with our lower self tend to push our buttons. The good news is that what annoys you about another is ultimately teaching you something about yourself.

What you hate in another you do yourself; it's the mirror in action and you can use this technique to weed out your controlling habits. Have you ever vented your frustrations to a friend and had them look at you and say they don't see the problem? This is because the behaviour that bothers you lives within you. That behaviour does not bother your friend because it does not live within them.

It seems incomprehensible that this could be so, but it is always true. What you hate in another you do yourself. A behaviour which annoys you does so because you are doing some version of it yourself, usually towards another person.

Find the lesson and set yourself free.

Lana

I met Lana for coffee after work. She could barely order without swearing at the waiter, she was so annoyed. She was working at her store's checkout when a customer complained there was a cotton thread pulled in the hem of the dress she was buying. The customer stood at the counter demanding 20 percent off the price. Lana said that it was a minor fault and she would get another one from the rack. The customer responded by snatching the dress from Lana's hands, throwing it at the rack, and walking out of the store yelling abuse.

I said to Lana, "You've had a really shit day." She said, "I know what you're going to say ... that what you hate in another you do yourself. But I just can't think about it right now." The next day Lana rang me and said, "Yes, I am snappy and walk out on my boyfriend. I attack him for the smallest reason, when I know I shouldn't."

I explained to her that she had a choice now. She was attracting these customers because she had the same behaviours within her. These events would stop when she addressed her beliefs controlling her behaviour towards her boyfriend.

Louise

Louise was chatting with a guy she met at a bar. After some time, he told her the reasons for his last relationship breaking up. He finished his story with: "She was wrong for what she did."

Immediately his comment triggered something within Louise. She was annoyed with how he condemned his ex. But she knew that what you hate in another you do yourself. She asked herself, "Who do I believe was wrong from my past?", and immediately her thoughts went to the guy who cheated on her multiple times. She was still angry with him.

But she also knew she wanted to stop attracting men who were resonating with the "wrongness belief" she was carrying about her ex.

Louise asked herself what else she could have done when she found him cheating. It was obvious to her now: kick him out and tell him never to return. She realised the annoyance she felt was towards herself for failing to take action.

Once she realised she was angry with herself, she had her power back. He might have cheated, and that is his karma, but it was her decision to stay each time, not his. She realised she had been like that her entire life, constantly giving second and third chances to people who didn't deserve it.

Her "aha moment" was when she realised she no longer needed to forgive her partner because there was nothing to forgive. Her ex had done her a favour; he had taught her it was time to release her habit of passivity.

Negative past life events can become empowering if we ask the right question, such as: "How am I attracting this into my life? Is there a pattern happening here? What in me is the same as in him? What part did I play in this situation?"

Examine each potential partner, and ask what is it in him which is replicating in you? If you have a habit of losing your temper, do you want to bring in a partner who replicates that, or are you willing to work on yourself to release that temper? How do you want your lessons: with a feather duster, a big stick or a sledgehammer? How do you want to learn to return to love?

Power

No one has the power to hurt you, ever, because you do not give them that power – anymore. Choose it that way. Forgiveness is not necessary when you realise they did not hurt you; they never could. It was only your mind which held onto the belief that you were hurt. What if you believed, "no one has the power to hurt me". In that moment you realise you are free.

As soon as you blame others, you stop learning. Blame causes you to repeat the past. Blame is also not sexy! It keeps you stuck in the past, stuck as the victim.

When you release blame, you release the need for forgiveness. Forgiveness does not mean that people are not responsible for their actions. Jail time or any karmic turnaround is theirs to deal with. But for you, finding there was nothing to forgive releases you from the invisible bond tying yourself to them.

You are your power source, you are love, you are strength, you have the power to change the world.

Justified resentment

Resentment is the feeling of bitterness you hold towards another. If you were subjected to violence or sexual abuse in your childhood, you would not be wrong in thinking that you are justified in holding onto your resentment.

Tina

When Tina was a teenager she was subjected to a sexual predator. It had taken courage for her to speak up and she reported the man for his actions. But the response she received was that she shouldn't have been wearing tight shorts and she should forget about the incident. Tina resented their response, but there was nothing she could do.

Many years later, she wrote about the incident in her journal, detailing every aspect she could remember, when she wrote, "I was betrayed by the person I made the report to, they failed to act." Immediately she had the realisation that betrayal was replicating its way through her life and into her own children's lives.

The past broke in that moment. She realised she would never stand by as the passive witness, brushing things under the carpet, keeping the peace whilst boyfriends and partners took advantage of her and overstepped their place in her children's lives, betraying her.

Over the years, Tina worked on forgiving the perpetrator and releasing the incident. But she never looked at the others involved. The people she had trusted to support her, to have her back; she didn't realise how much she resented them and how she felt betrayed by a system which let her down.

Release resentment from your life. Find the hidden feelings which are attracting your partners.

Judging events

One of the behaviours attracting our partners is the meaning we create from events. We love looking for meaning in everything that happens around us. We love to label and pigeonhole people's behaviour. We ask, why did they say that? What did they mean by that? We read meaning into our friends' and our partner's texts, into emails we receive from work colleagues and associates. Our mind loops around all of the possible connotations, none of which may be true.

The problem with assigning a meaning and a label to everything is that it changes how we interact with people. If our partner does not text us very often one day or one week, we may choose the meaning that he doesn't love us anymore.

The belief that he doesn't love us anymore changes everything we do and say. All because we created a false meaning; all because he was busy and couldn't send a text. From that moment onwards, with every conversation, every outing, every event, we will have the tinted glasses on, shading our whole interaction.

One reason we need to read meaning into everything is our need for certainty. We would rather be certain that a meaning is negative, than be uncertain about what was meant. We seem to have inherited a habit of assuming the worst. I read once that before antiseptic and ready access to medical help, a small injury such as a cut could bring death. Our minds, therefore, have been hardwired to judge unknown events as having negative outcomes.

Instead of judging events, use the signs, clear your mind of thoughts and check in with your inner wisdom. Ask yourself, "What is the truth behind these events? What is it that I need to know? What is it about this event which may relate to another part of my life?"

Then go for a walk, have a shower, find an activity to relax you and release your mind from talking to you, so the wisdom of the small still voice within you can show you the truth.

Sarah

Sarah: I've just received a text from a friend. I can't understand why she sent it. I'm not well at the moment and this text has made me so annoyed. I'm fuming, actually.

Me: Okay, anger always leads to the wrong path. Let's take your friend out of the picture and look at your life. Who do you attack in your life?

Sarah: I get angry with my sister and I don't let her express herself before jumping to conclusions and jumping down her throat.

Me: Therefore, your friend's text is for the benefit of you and your sister. If you can derive learning from the text, you can fuel change in your life for the better.

Sarah: Okay, I will find the learning. This new way of looking at the situation makes me feel better, and empowered to do better with my sister. So what about dealing with the text?

Me: Well, for now the text upsets you. Ask the universe to lift the anger and annoyance from you, and send forgiveness to yourself and your friend as you cannot forgive her now.

Sarah: Thank you, this is making me feel better.

The interpreting mind uses the offence it sees in text messages as justification to lash out. An hour later or the next day when your wise self has returned, you might realise you over-reacted, but it is too late. Trust has been destroyed.

Texting in anger never resolves anything and cuts someone out of your life who may be your future loyal friend.

Prayer: Please universe, I ask for the consequences of this situation to be undone for everyone's highest life. I ask for wisdom and light to enfold all involved and return them to love.

YOU are not your mind. There is always a higher meaning.

Certainty

Have you ever been annoyed in traffic after someone has cut you off? Have you then walked into work affirming to everyone, "It's going to be one of those days", thereby cementing your day into a "bad day". Then you go home to your partner and you continue that bad day with them.

It becomes a self-fulfilling prophecy. You allow your mind to turn one incident into your fate. If you had a bad morning, why would you want the afternoon to be the same? The past was bad enough; why manifest it in the present?

The reason again lies in our need for certainty. Choosing that the rest of the day, or the rest of your life, fulfils some negative premonition that "nothing good ever happens to me; I'll never find anyone" gives you a kind of certainty for what lies ahead.

Being certain about a bad future can feel better than feeling uncertain about a positive future. We feel safe when we are certain, even when the expected outcome is negative. Our belief that someone does not like us gives us certainty and makes us feel safe, even if it's not true.

I stand in my certainty that I have my back.

Creativity

Why is uncertainty a problem? Because when we are uncertain, our mind's creative aspect takes over. It makes up stories based upon unlimited negative possibilities. If you ever think that you are not creative, just look at the negative assumptions your mind can make up in less than a second.

Our mind needs a job.[1] It needs a purpose. It craves creativity. If you do not find a creative outlet for your mind, it will seek its creativity in destructive ways, through its habit of interpreting events negatively.

Knowing that every opportunity is a learning experience changes your perception about what daily life is about. In any stressful moment, ask yourself, what is this teaching me? This question returns you to your power.

We often judge ourselves as not creative, because we believe that only artistic people are creative. But creativity can be found in all aspects of your life: in your problem-solving ability at work, in the way you decorate your house, in the way you plant your garden, in your social media account. The opportunities to be creative are endless.

So, if you find yourself judging what everyone says, looking for meaning in their words, then stop and look around your life. Are you doing anything that fulfils your need for creativity?

You are not here to live small. You are not here to allow

---

[1] Elizabeth Gilbert, *'Big Magic'*.

others to dominate you. You are here to grow and move into creativity, thrive and shine within your life.

I allow myself to express my creative flow.

Morning routine

We live our life according to what we believe, and one way to transform our life is to start each day with our new positive future locked into our cells. One way to do this is to create a morning routine based on certainty. Each morning I get up and dance my affirmations, my positive motivation for my day and for my life, the reason why I do what I do. This creates certainty for my day ahead and ensures I start the day focused on where I'm going, not on where I've been.

The morning routine creates steady change. Opportunities and synchronicities start to occur. The right person appears at the right time; life starts falling into place. Manifesting your dreams becomes easier, all through adding a three and a half minute change to your day.

I am my own champion. I create my own miracle life. I believe in me.

Morning routine exercise[2]

In the morning as soon as you get up, put on your motivational song. Find an upbeat song, that you love. You are going to use all of your senses to embody certainty

---

2   I acknowledge my coach John Sader for encouraging me to make the morning routine a part of my daily life and to Jean Houston for first teaching me this exercise.

through sound and movement. You are going to affirm, sing or yell your affirmations whilst dancing around the room.

You may need to find somewhere in the house away from everyone else. Others may doubt what you are doing, but the proof is the change you will see in the following weeks and months.

As you verbalise your affirmations, see them, feel them, imagine them as if they are real, right now.

Mine go something like this: I am an author, I am a teacher, I am love, I am light, I am healthy, I meditate daily, I inspire change, etc.

Perceptions

Our minds are expert at making up stories based on what we perceive, primarily through what we see and hear. This makes our mind's perception unreliable. We don't ask questions before drawing conclusions. Our mind springs into action, making up a story based on itself as the only witness, as the only source of knowledge.

Imagine you are watching football on TV. You see a player hit by an opponent's elbow and fall to the ground. You yell at the TV, "Send him off!" The TV then flashes up a second camera angle that shows the player tripped and the opponent's elbow missed him. Your assumption to send him off was wrong. The first camera created your perception.

Imagine you see someone walking across the street. They appear to be glaring at you. You think, "you bitch", but in reality, they don't have their contacts in and can't even see you.

Your perceptions take you hostage. False perceptions drop your vibration, destroying your happy state. This negative state then guides your actions. You create accusations in your head, and your mood changes.

When you feel that negative state take you hostage, tell your mind to stand down. If you can drop down into your heart space and deep breathe for a few seconds your mind can reset. Once reset you, the being who lives within your body, can take control and allow wisdom and clarity to guide you on the way forward.

Remind your mind: He didn't text. That's it. He didn't bring you flowers. That's it. There is no story to make up about these facts. But you can ask the universe to show you the truth behind these actions. Ask for a sign. Then release the belief that these actions have any ability to hurt you.

Question your perceptions; is there another way of looking at this? Can I be sure that what I believe is true? Is there another higher perspective? Is there a deeper understanding that I am missing here? How is the past repeating? Ask the universe: please show me the truth behind these actions. Thank you for sending me a sign.

Ask the universe. Show me the truth behind these actions. Thank you for sending me a sign.

Regret

Regret keeps us stuck in the past. The past only exists according to how we remember it. Our perception of the past may differ from that of another person who witnessed it. Therefore, our version of the past does not serve us, except to keep us stuck.

Regret also stops us from living in the now, which is where our power lies. Choose instead to release the grip regret has on you, keeping you stuck repeating the past. Learn from your mistakes; use the feedback you have received from your mistakes to manifest a present based on your highest purpose.

Ask the universe: Show me my new path forward.

We are right

The mind is constantly on the lookout for proof that it is right. We base our actions and accusations on what we believe to be right. What we do not realise is that everyone else is doing the same thing. They are basing their actions on what they believe to be right.

If we go into every argument believing we are right, how can we ever learn why the other person believes they are right? Have you ever thought, I wonder why he believes he is right? What hurt in him is showing up? What hurt in me is showing up through this argument?

Perhaps the mind feels it needs to justify its own existence or importance. It is never able to escape the confines of the head, never able to feel, touch or taste anything. It is dependent on the rest of the body for information. If the mind does not influence you, it has no power. And the mind is always trying to show its power.

Think about how this plays out in world events. Why are people fighting overseas? Why does each side believe they are right? It does not mean that you agree with them. It just means that life is not always black and white, and our perception of any situation may not be the one that will bring peace. Remember, the mind will dismiss the truth in favour of the version it has made up, if you do not question it.

Ask yourself, what if both sides are right?

Our mind, friend or foe

Our mind, unless trained, is always looking for a way to keep itself occupied and entertained. Bored and wanting to be right, attacking others can be its tool of choice and its choice of entertainment.

Give your mind direction. Set it on the path of what you desire. Your mind is a powerful tool. It gets you to appointments, it organises your finances, it works out what you need to fill the fridge, it works out how to take care of others, etc.

As the owner of your mind, your job is to focus it towards what you want. You, the person who lives in your body, directs your mind, not the other way around. The mind is your tool. You are not its tool, living out a life of its choosing.

Ask, how can I create a better life? How can I bring more peace into my life? Where can I make a difference today?

My mind is a tool; it works for me.

Be vigilant

When we start a new activity, new job, new college, our mind becomes a fertile playground for making up stories. It is easy to slip into negative assumptions. The mind will go back to what it knows: its old negative habit of interpreting events negatively.

Some years ago, I started dance lessons. In class one day, I saw my teacher, whilst looking at me, cover her mouth and speak to her assistant. Straightaway my mind said, she is talking about me. My mind then said, what am I doing here? Why did I think I could do this? My happy state left me, and anxiety was in its place.

Finally, I woke up from my thoughts. My mind had just run off with the truth. I was stunned at how swiftly my mind reduced three seconds into the uncertainty and anxiety I was now feeling. It had been years since I had experienced my mind making up negative stories, but a new environment was all that was required for my mind to leap back into its old habit.

The truth was I knew nothing about what she was saying. Perhaps she was hungry or she was telling her assistant about the next step she needed to teach us. Even if she was talking about me, it was her business, nothing to do with me.

In learning how to dance, I was in unfamiliar territory, with new people, learning something I had never done before. My mind was uncertain about who these people were, and that uncertainty was all my mind needed to slip into negativity. Be awake when dealing with new people if your mind reverts to "stranger danger". This was a message we learnt as children to keep us safe. Be aware when your mind starts giving you negative feedback when you are in new situations with new people.

Your negative mind is the alert for YOU to take control. Ask, what is the higher truth here? What am I learning?

Beliefs

Our beliefs choose our partners and our life events. A belief is something that the mind has accepted is true. A belief can be created in an instant. In that small half-second we see someone looking at us strangely, without any further evidence, we can decide that person doesn't like us. As quick as that a new belief is created: "He doesn't like me."

We are constantly creating new beliefs and looking for evidence that those beliefs are true. Our willingness to release our beliefs, that they are the truth in our lives, is part of our journey to freedom. Socrates said, "The only true wisdom is in knowing you know nothing." Your old beliefs have created your life up to now; open yourself up to new beliefs.

When you hold a belief as true, such as he doesn't like me, it skews every conversation you have. Every encounter with him then comes from the mindset that you are trying to get him to like you. What this does is take you out of the present and into some fantasy that you have created. Whether someone likes you or not is actually not your business. Your business is to show up, being the best person you can be in any given moment.

Each time we add a new negative belief into our body, it is added to our existing disempowering beliefs created in our childhood. It was in our childhood and in our teenage years that we found ourselves at our most vulnerable, when we didn't have the skill set to check whether a belief was going to enhance our lives or create future pain.

I can change the "truisms" in my life.

Belief shifting

You have lived your old life based on your beliefs; you have learnt the lessons that these beliefs brought you. Your old, limited beliefs, such as: I am not enough; I am unworthy; I am not lovable; I am not good enough; I must punish myself. These beliefs do not serve you except to draw into your life events, boyfriends, partners, friends, workplace experiences that match those beliefs. (Some beliefs sound similar, such as "I'm not good enough" and "I am not enough", but each carries a different weight within your psyche.)

Now is the time to create new beliefs and fulfil your potential by choosing beliefs based on love. Each and every day you have the opportunity to release disempowering beliefs. Consider whether elite athletes could achieve what hasn't been done before if they held the belief it was impossible. An elite athlete creates a new belief about what he or she can do well before they actually do it. Another example is scientists looking for breakthroughs in their field. If they held the belief that a new outcome was not possible, then humankind would never have made it to the moon and we wouldn't have electricity.

My life past was based on my old beliefs. My life future is based on beliefs which empower me.

Therapies

I have worked with many alternative therapies over the years and have read a library of books, and the common realisation is that we can release our disempowering beliefs just as easily as we can bring in new beliefs.

We know how we create a negative belief. It is by accepting something as true. But how do we release a negative belief? There are many alternative therapies, such as kinesiology, tapping, ThetaHealing®, a technique created by Vianna Stibal, *The Work* by Byron Katie, and Rapid Transformational Therapy™ (RTT™) by Marisa Peer, as well as life coaches, that can assist you in releasing disempowering beliefs.

I've felt empowered by many of these therapies and have gone on to train in alternative therapies myself. Find your own path, whether you are drawn to an alternative therapist, psychologist or counsellor. Find the one, or the many, that work for you. At the back of this book, I have a list of further reading to propel you on your journey to create an inspired life.

I can create new beliefs based on love.

Affirmations

We do not just retain a belief in our mind. A single belief can be felt throughout our entire body. You only have to feel anger to know your whole body is affected, or feel the happiness in knowing that "everyone loves me".

One of my favourite ways to bring in new knowing (belief) or release a disempowering thought is to use the energy of the moonlight. With this process you remember that you are made up of cells and atoms, that light can flow in and through you, along with the energies of the new belief, your new positive affirmation, your new knowing.

Whilst standing in the moonlight, ask yourself what are you believing that no longer serves your highest good? Then, allow any thoughts that put you down to release from you, to float up into the moonlight.

Imagine that the physical, mental and emotional effects of the belief also lift from you. You may feel or sense it lifting from your body up through your shoulders and out the top of your head. Sometimes you may sense a blackness, like a sticky tar containing all the emotions, lifting from you.

I repeat my positive affirmations to myself and as the moonlight shines down on me, I imagine those new knowings coming down in the moonlight, in and through me. I allow the new energies to absorb in and through me. I have found profound changes occur after doing this simple technique.

You might ask, what if there isn't any moonlight? Sometimes, when I'm doing a yoga pose, I imagine the moonlight above me and my positive affirmations absorbing in and through my entire being. Basically, you can do it anywhere, but the moonlight is useful to help you focus your mind on what you are doing.

I am loved. I am joy. I am the change I want to see in others.

The six core knowings

By knowing the below as truth, you can feel your life transform. These knowings ground you on this earth; they can make you feel that you belong, and that is powerful. You may insert brother and sister or other significant person along with your parents.

I am loved

I am love

I am enough

I am safe

My mum/dad is proud of me

My mum/dad approves of me

Proud

We have often lived our lives striving to make our parents proud of us, to have our parents love us. This striving prevents us from fully standing in our power, and knowing ourselves as amazing, magnificent, loving people.

What if you just created a new knowing within your soul: "My mum/dad is proud of me", or "My mum/dad loves me"?

Meditation: Knowing exercise

My parents (insert mum/dad) are proud of me.

Sit down and move into a relaxed state; imagine you are in the moonlight. Close your eyes and make up a scene where you see your parents smiling, telling you they are proud of you. Stay there for a moment and feel the love. Inside of them, within their true self, they love you and they are proud of you. Feel it, stay there, relax into this knowing.

All their life it has been their personality which has been blocking them from showing and telling you that they are proud of you. Know that your parents are proud of you and that they love you. Stay in this joy, knowing it to be true. When you are ready, stretch open your eyes, have a drink of water and have a great day.

You can use this knowing exercise for the six core knowings or any belief or knowing you are missing in your life.

My parents are proud of me.

Disappointment

We can feel disappointed when an outcome occurs which does not meet our expectation. When the disappointment emotion grips us, it can block change and prevent us from speaking up. I can trace all the things I've been disappointed in back to the root cause: "Did I speak up, did I say what I wanted and did I stick to it?"

When disappointment sets in, we often look at the other person as the cause and not ourself. Similar to blame, we shift the focus from ourselves and place it on the person over there. You want them to change and them to do it right. But they do what they do in accordance with their values and beliefs.

Disappointment is an opportunity for you to reframe your thoughts and change your actions. You can use disappointment as a message to you from your body that you are off course with your thinking.

You can become disappointed that he never arranged

anything for Valentine's Day, that he forgot your anniversary. Disappointment can overtake your life. But disappointment disempowers us, and it means that someone else has control over our happiness.

When you feel disappointed, ask: "What is the truth in this situation? What am I learning here? Did I articulate what I wanted? Did I set my boundaries? Did I ignore my gut? Do I have my own back?"

Change "I am disappointed" to "I have gained wisdom through this experience; this experience has made me stronger and has given me insight into what to do next time. I have strengthened my resolve to follow my gut instinct."

Never label anything as disappointment again; it is a waste of your emotional energy. Reframe it and thrive.

I have control over my happiness. I follow my gut instinct.

Speaking up

Many of us learnt from childhood that it was not safe to speak up. As we grew older and tried to find our voice, further negative events reinforced the pattern, creating a lifelong habit. Your friends may see you as confident and in charge of your life. However, when you are dealing with someone in authority, a work colleague or a tradesperson, suddenly you may revert back in your old habit of not speaking up.

This is exacerbated by another habit – avoiding confrontation. When we believe that confrontation creates negative consequences, we passively live life, trying not to offend anyone, all the while silencing our own voice.

To avoid confrontation, we ask polite, tentative questions of our partners and others to satisfy our mind that we haven't offended them. Passive questions and statements such as "Would you like to ... take the trash out?", "Could you ...?", "Perhaps we could ...", instead of speaking directly and saying what we want.

Think back through your past and imagine if you had exercised that muscle – speaking up – how easy would you find it today? That's all it is, an unused muscle, something you have never used – your voice. Over and over, you will find the universe sends you people and situations teaching you how to speak up.

Train your brain and body to feel comfortable speaking up through visualisation. Sit or lie down and visualise the times where you did not speak up. Now change the past and see yourself speaking confidently with a positive outcome.

Then vision yourself in the future, speaking to people who respect you and whom you respect, with confidence, laughing and feeling good about speaking up. Vision yourself in a relationship being respected, speaking with confidence. See the other person nodding, listening to you, smiling and hugging you at the end.

Take small steps in safe environments to create your new habit of speaking up, maybe with a shop assistant or at the hairdresser. In difficult situations, ask how you can create a positive outcome for yourself and the other person. Ask the universe what is your best way forward to overcome this habit of not speaking up, and then watch out for the opportunity as the universe sends it your way.

I trust myself. I have faith in myself. I speak with grace and ease.

Events

When we are stuck in the past, we allow minor issues to turn into tsunamis. Leaving clothes on the floor, not putting away the shopping, leaving keys on the table turn into all-out war in the house.

Those are just events. You were not bothered the first time they happened. You may have said, "Honey, I've put the keys in the jar so you don't lose them." The twentieth time you find his keys lying around, you pick them up and hurl them at the jar. You are pissed off and your peace is disturbed.

But you have a choice. Continue to complain, yell and get agitated, or find a new solution. Choice is looking at events from a new angle. What could this situation be teaching you? How could you see this differently? Is this just a childhood pattern replaying in your adult life? Is this event triggering something from your past?

We go through life thinking that life is happening to us, instead of realising it's happening for us, helping us to step up and break free from our lifelong habits. We forget that we are co-creators in this lifetime. We are not at the mercy of someone else; we are at the mercy of our inner self, who is crying out for us to step up and be the people we were meant to be.

There is only ever the here and now. The past is gone.

Laura

One summer's day when Laura was six, she was out walking with her older sisters and her cousins. Her sister was the school captain and studied hard as she wanted to be a doctor.

The older cousins were joking around, slinging off insults and one-liners at each other. Laura wanted to get in on the action and say something clever. She waited until there was a gap and then made her debut. "Shut up!", she said.

Her sister spun around, and pointed her finger at Laura's face and said, "You don't speak to me like that!" The air went silent. Tears welled up, but Laura held them in. Her older sister's disapproval cut like a knife. Hurt and disappointed, Laura never spoke up again. This was the start of a lifelong pattern with people in authority.

When Laura was 25, she bumped into a guy from high school whom she had a crush on when she was 16. He had moved away after finishing high school. They went for coffee and talked for hours. Laura could feel herself falling for him again.

A few weeks later, as serendipity would have it, Laura bumped into her teenage crush. He was back in town, helping his father build an extension on their family home. Laura, her heart bubbling with joy, blurted out whatever popped into her head: what had he been up to, where had he been, how long was he in town, who had he been out with …

He looked at her coldly, and said, "I thought you weren't like those other girls." Then turned his back, jumped in his car and roared up the road.

Her mind raced. She hadn't meant to offend him, how could she be so stupid, oh, why didn't she think before she spoke? She walked back into her friend's house, tears welling in her eyes.

His words tormented her and cemented her to a lifelong pattern of not speaking up. Never did she question her mind or his behaviour. She could have asked, "What the hell's wrong with him?" Instead, she presumed it was her fault. She may have been the catalyst for his behaviour, but she was not responsible for his response; he was. She allowed a ten-second encounter to change how she would respond in future relationships.

The universe gave Laura a second chance 15 years later. She had been with her partner for three years. They talked about getting married and having children, but something always prevented them. Eventually she said to him, "I feel like I'm stagnating." Insulted, he said to her, "Well, if I'm inconveniencing you and blocking your life's dream, I'll leave right now." She watched him pack his things and walk out, doing the same as her old crush had done, slamming the door behind him. But this time she watched with wiser eyes. She saw his behaviour as childish. It was not her problem if he wanted to walk out. His actions were his responsibility.

Always ask yourself, would you do that? Would you react that way? If loving communication results in the other person walking out, then make the conscious decision that you've dodged a bullet. He has shown you who he is on a bad day. Our power lies in the conclusions we draw from events.

Choose an empowering belief from the events around you, and life will start to transform.

Clearing negative events screen technique

Our memories that are vivid in sensory detail have more power in keeping the past alive. Often we remember people's words and their tone as clearly as the day they said them, as clear as if we were watching a movie behind our eyes.

Think back through your strong memories. Do you remember the colours, sounds or the tone of the voices? We can change the impact of negative memories by reframing them into black and white, and by changing the sounds of voices that hurt or upset us into squeaking sounds.

My coach taught me this technique and I've expanded on it to recreate a new past. After all, you've experienced the old past. Why not give yourself an empowering past memory to help propel you into the future? The past doesn't exist anywhere but in your memory. We can create an empowering past to fuel a positive present.

Laura clearing the past example[3]

Laura closes her eyes and imagines a movie screen. Her first crush is there, talking to her on the footpath. She turns the scene into black and white and changes the sound of his voice into a squeaking mouse. He walks away and she shrinks the scene in her mind's eye down to a small dot. She repeats three times.

She repeats again, but this time she's standing behind

---

3   Acknowledging my coach John Sader.

herself, watching herself as if there were two of her. She watches herself change the scene to black and white, change his voice, then shrinks the scene into a dot. She repeats three times.

She creates a new ending.

Laura again watches the scene in black and white, shrinking it down as he leaves. The screen then comes back to colour and she sees herself jumping for joy. "What the hell's wrong with him? Thank God he's gone. I can do better! Thank you universe for sending me someone better!" In vivid colour, she sees herself jumping for joy, free to move on! She repeats this new ending three times.

Meditation: Clearing negative events

Do not attempt to clear a severely traumatic event; choose a minor event.

Close your eyes. Start your relaxed, even breathing. Imagine you can see a movie screen in your mind's eye. On that screen, you are watching the scene you wish to clear.

Change the scene to black and white. Change any harsh or attacking voices to the sound of a squeaking talking mouse. Then, shrink your movie screen down to a dot, and let it disappear. Open your eyes. Repeat three times.

Now this time, when you see the screen, imagine you see yourself sitting watching the screen. You are watching yourself clear the event. See yourself watching the screen turn to black and white. Change any harsh or attacking voices to the sound of a squeaking talking mouse. Then, shrink your movie screen down to a dot, and let it disappear. Open your eyes. Repeat three times.

> Empowering ending:
>
> Now put a new, empowering ending to an event on your movie screen to help propel you forward into a new future. Choose a new past. Say, for example, you constantly found yourself silent and never speaking up. See yourself on your screen able to speak up clearly and confidently with the love and respect of the people around you.

Problems follow you

Many women have escaped from a violent or domineering family home, only to marry the same personality they were running from. Leaving is important, but escaping into the arms of another is not the complete solution. Unresolved problems will follow you, whether in your personal life or your working life.

Angela left her job because she felt her boss was too pushy and did not respect her. She did not speak up before she left to clear the air, or resolve within herself how she was attracting this situation. Some months later, she started a new job, and within a few months she was having the same problems with her new boss.

Blaming your old boss or your previous partner takes away your responsibility. You deny that you had a part to play or, even worse, you deny that you had something empowering to learn. Unresolved business will follow you. If you can find the part you played, no matter how small, you will have access to learning something which will empower you.

In repeating events, you are the common denominator; use that knowledge to your advantage. Never let a moment slip to question repeating events. Ask yourself, what is this situation teaching you? What empowering new learning can you take from the situation to propel you into an inspired future.

Ask the universe, what am I learning here, what do I need to know?

Stuck in negativity

Do you find yourself constantly talking to friends about what someone did to you five, ten or more years ago? Do bitterness, revenge and resentment dominate your thoughts, emotions and conversations? If so, you are stuck in negativity.

Imagine you met a guy at a bar and all he talked about was how bad his life was, and how his ex did him wrong? You would avoid him. He is telling you what you need to know to assess who he is. He is holding on to resentment and using blame as a way to stay stuck.

I read somewhere that we drink the poison and expect the other person to die. The poison is our negativity. Do not be the person you are trying to avoid from chapter one. Otherwise, you will attract new partners who carry the same baggage, who mirror your negative aspects. Being negative is a pattern, and left unchecked it will dominate your life. Like attracts like. Be the change you want to see in a new partner.

Be the person you want your new partner to be.

Meditation: Daily grounding

Grounding is a way to reset your energy and connect you to the earth as well as the wisdom from above.

Find a comfortable sitting position, whether the floor or a chair. Close your eyes and relax, and calmly, rhythmically breathe. Breathe in, 1-2-3-4, breathe out, 1-2-3-4. Relax down into your chair and breathe to the number beat that suits you. Make it the same in and out relaxed, calm, even breath.

Imagine yourself going deep down into the centre of the earth. You can visualise the centre of the earth as being a warm, welcoming space with crystals, or just visualise a sign saying centre of the earth. Imagine the healing energy of the earth is gently rising up through your feet, to your legs, up around your torso, through your neck and into your head. You feel strong, relaxed and connected to the earth.

Now imagine a gold cord connected to the top of your head. Follow this cord up and past the sky and the planets. The cord connects you to the wisdom of the universe, and all around you is the golden gridwork of the universe. Allow yourself to sense the golden light of the universe passing in and through you. All of you is connected to the wisdom of the universe.

See all around you sparkling light. Sense the colour of this light and allow it to flow in and through you; in through your head, down your neck, into your shoulders, your arms, your upper body, your lower body, down through your legs, until your entire being is flowing with this beautiful light.

Remember your feet are connected to the wisdom of the earth. Feel that connection.

Now imagine your day ahead, invigorated by the energy of mother

TRANSFORMATION

earth drawing up into you, bringing wisdom, clarity and joy to all you do today. See yourself laughing and smiling as you go about your day.

When you are ready, slowly open your eyes, wriggle your toes and feet, stretch, have a drink of water, look around the room and have a great day!

Highlights

- Your mind can be your best friend and ally.
- Labelling events as negative, leads to pain.
- Always question your mind when it has assumed a negative position.
- Ask the universe to show you the truth in any situation.
- What you hate in another you do yourself.
- People will show up in your life to show you where you have moved away from love.
- Holding on to resentment can block repeating patterns from being revealed to you.
- You can release your disempowering beliefs.
- Accept empowering truths about yourself.
- Create new beliefs based on love.
- Disappointment tells you your expectation was not met. It prevents you from speaking up. Reframe disappointment into, "I have gained wisdom from this situation."
- New habits are like weak muscles; it is practice that strengthens them.
- Create new positive habits. Vision yourself at night before going to bed, speaking confidently amongst your peers, amongst people in authority. See them reacting positively to you.

❦ Reflections ❦

1. Clean up your bedroom and closet.
2. Declutter, repaint, repair existing furniture or purchase new furniture.
3. Throw out or donate clothing you have not worn in the past 12 months that you will likely not wear again.

Self-reflection questions

1. Look back over your life and contemplate who might be in pain because of you.

Send love and ask the universe to heal the past and allow everyone involved to move forward on their highest path.

2. What you hate in another you do yourself.

- Take a piece of paper and draw one line down the middle of the page.
- Write a heading in the first column: "I hate that he/she ..." Write everything down that you hate; don't censor yourself.
- Write a heading in the second column: "My reflections." Then ask yourself, where have you repeated some version of the behaviour found in column one, either with a partner, a friend, a sibling, a co-worker or parent? Where have you shown up in your life as the person you've written about in column one?
- On another page, list the repeating events you find in "My reflections" column.
- What lesson can you learn? What empowered action can you create? Are you being taught to stand in your power? Do you want to keep using relationships as a tool for learning these things? What hobby, new career path or friendship group can motivate you to learn in ways which will uplift you?

Moonlight affirmations

I allow creativity into my life.
I allow myself to express my creativity.
I am creative.
I allow myself to be confident.
I can be confident.
I am confident.
I can ask questions.
I can ask questions safely.
I allow myself to be respected.
I can be respected in my workplace.
I am respected.
I can respect myself.
I can discern my boyfriend's words.
I can release the fear of being rejected.
I now release the expectation of being rejected.
I can now live my life without rejecting others.
I can allow joy into my life.
I can allow love into my life.
I am love.
I am joy.

CHAPTER 5

EVOLVING

> "Your task is not to seek for love, but merely to seek and find all the barriers within yourself that you have built against it."
> — Rumi

There is a future waiting for you to show up. When you spend your time fixated on the past or fixated on a fearful future, you delay manifesting a life filled with love and joy. You can lay blame on others, hoping that the pain you feel inside might ease.

Our little self lives in pain and wants others to be in the same pain. Inflicting our little self on others drives them to their little self, creating a never-ending circle. But taking responsibility and finding success from suffering, victory from victimhood, we lay the seeds to thrive.

Healing starts at home and begins with you. World change starts at home and begins with you. Your ultimate life starts at home and begins with you.

You are the change you seek in a partner.

Your first steps

Whilst reading this chapter, examine your wardrobe. Do your clothing choices reflect who you want to be? Are you still dressing like a child or like you did ten years ago? How does your hairstyle or colour reflect where you are wanting to take your life?

Think about where you want to be in the next five years. Close your eyes and imagine what you are doing, where you are, how you speak. Now look at your clothing and hairstyle. What changes can you make to bring that person of the future into your life now?

Stephanie

During the school holidays, Stephanie, who was 15, would meet her friends at her local café for lunch. One day, whilst she waited for her friends down the back in the corner booth, a family acquaintance walked in. He was older and wasn't her friend, so she didn't take any notice of him. He walked behind her as if he was on his way to the restroom. Instead, he stopped, bent down across her, put his hand on her shoulder and moved his fingers into her blouse. With the tips of his fingers, he pushed under her bra whilst whispering, how does that make you feel? His other hand then moved onto her leg.

Stephanie froze, gripping the edge of her seat. From the corner of her eye, she saw the restroom door swing open and a customer walk out. Her molester stood up, but he kept his hand pressing down on her shoulder, preventing her from moving. He then strode out of the restaurant, as if he had just closed a business deal.

That evening, Stephanie told her mother. Without emotion, her mother replied that there are things we women must endure. Stephanie wanted to scream "no", but being only 15, it wasn't something she could argue with her mother about; it was embarrassing enough just to even tell her.

Her mother was active in many clubs and charities, which caused Stephanie to encounter her molester at events. He would corner Stephanie, wanting to know if she had a boyfriend and asked other personal questions which made her skin crawl. She learnt to create excuses and diversions to avoid his questions. Eventually, she moved away from home and away from her molester.

For 20 years, Stephanie did not hear his voice again, until her mother was in hospital. Someone had called him, and by chance, he was walking out of her mother's room as she arrived. He looked as good as ever, still fit, hair greying on both sides of his face. With that same confidence he'd always had, he said, "How are you? I hear you've separated from your husband."

Stephanie froze; she hated dealing with his intrusive questions. Her daughter, Chloe, later asked, "Who was that guy?" Stephanie had had enough of secrets and told her daughter the whole story.

Some weeks later, Stephanie's molester phoned her. He had obtained her number from her mother under the excuse of wanting to help Stephanie rearrange her finances. Stephanie declined his help by saying she was busy or wasn't available to meet at the time he proposed. She said everything, except no.

Stephanie's daughter Chloe was a teenager and she had

a voice. Sick of him calling, she answered the phone and said, "Mum is not interested in your financial planning, stop calling, and f--- off." He never called again.

Stephanie believed there was a higher purpose for what she went through. The universe was asking her to find her voice, to stand up and speak up. Repeatedly, she chose the role of the pacifier, the peacemaker, instead of saying what she wanted.

This man thought he had the right to enquire about her personal life because she did not speak up. Predators do not understand basic values of morality and decency. Treating a predator with the same respect you treat a friend does not work. Stephanie's family pattern was to keep the peace, to be the quiet person who did not rock the boat, to be the person who did not stand out in a crowd. Stephanie chose her mother's path, which was to be silent.

A predator has no desire to keep the peace or they would not do what they do. Their values say it is okay to touch and abuse someone else's child.

The universe is asking us to step out of our comfort zone. Being aware of your values is crucial to setting your boundaries, especially with those who abuse their power. You will attract unequal relationships until you consciously know and live your values.

Fixing others

You can distract yourself from your life by focusing your attention on fixing other people. Your mind can use this tactic to distract you from your fear of failure. Failure is normal. Failure resets your course, or tells you that your method needs changing. We would have no new inventions if inventors gave up on their first attempt.

Unconsciously, we can seek out partners who need fixing as this enables us to feel valued, to feel love. It feels good to help someone. However, love and value yourself where you are on your journey. You can then love and value others where they are on their journey. You allow them to make their mistakes, just as you allow yourself.

When people are ready to change, they will seek you out. Until then, you are the friend who listens, not the one who fixes or gives constant advice. Listen to others without jumping in to speak each time they take a breath. Create a new habit, focus on what uplifts you, what gives you a sense of creativity and purpose.

I focus my attention on my life. I love and value myself.

Searching for you

We are often searching for ourselves unconsciously. We want to feel who we are and, without realising it, we search for who we are through our dating life.

When we don't value ourselves we can look to boyfriends and partners to provide our value in life. We can neglect our own families and seek purpose and fulfilment through our partners' lives.

Who are you avoiding loving in this lifetime? Is there someone in your family who is craving your love and attention?

Check in with yourself. Do you seek out partners with

problems as a way of finding your value? If you can be valuable to them you must be valuable to yourself. But when you try to be of value to someone else, you often choose someone who actually doesn't value you.

You must value yourself first. Your search is over; the person you have been looking for to value you is you.

I am love. I am found.

Responsibility

We can feel responsible for our partners' and our friends' happiness and wellbeing. This is especially the case when we have children. We want them to be happy and have a better life than we did.

Feeling responsible for others is a habit which does not serve us. It disempowers others and prevents us from taking the right action. Sometimes a person needs to struggle and reach their own answers, without having well-meaning advice thrown at them. When you want to offer help, offer an ear to listen, to help them to be heard.

Ask them questions to stimulate their own thought process and find their own solution-based process, without trying to give them your version of the answers. Epiphanies come from your own realisations. Remember, you have not lived their life or walked their path, so your advice, although well-meaning may not be the solution that they need. Sometimes the best advice you can give is to shine within your own life.

It is our right to have control over our own lives. When people lose control of their life they can rebel in unhealthy ways, using addictions, illnesses and other problems to break free.

We cannot take away another's responsibility for their life, but we can be the light that shows them the way.

Wishing them bad

My grandmother told me a story about how two tradesmen came to her house, each for separate jobs. Both of them overcharged her and did a shoddy job. She said she never wished them ill, but ill events did come to them. We'd call that "their karma" these days.

We love to tell stories about what our ex did to us. We love to talk about how bad they were, how they ruined us financially, how they did not take any interest in our kids. Our friends agree and they repeat our stories. This constant angst and resentment keeps your mind and energy tied to your past partner, blocking their karma.[1]

Each time you complain and speak with anger about your ex, your body is getting a dose of that hatred. When you use these stories to make yourself the victim you are keeping yourself locked in the past.

What happened is over, it is in the past, unless you choose to keep it alive. Whether your ex ran off with your best friend, took you to the cleaners, or is sitting in the sun on a beach, sipping cocktails, enjoying himself with his latest fling. It is over. Being angry poisons your cells with hatred, and if you have children, they grow up learning this pattern from you.

---

1   Doreen Virtue, "I Can Do It!" seminar, Melbourne, 2011.

If you are constantly talking about how someone has "done you wrong", ask yourself, what is the payoff? What benefit are you getting from repeating your story? Is it sympathy? What is the benefit of focusing on the past? Are you addicted to being the victim? Victims are not sexy, the victorious are. You are no longer the victim. You are victorious.

When your focus is on the resentment and anger from the past, you keep yourself stuck. The path to success is found by focusing on your life.

Every time you think about your ex, remind yourself, "There is a solution to this, I just don't know it yet. There is a way forward for everyone's highest path ... thank you for sending me the best way forward, (universe)."

I choose to thrive within my own life. I now focus on creating an empowered life for me.

Endings

When a relationship has ended, see your ex-partner happy. Imagine them in a bubble moving forward and living a better life. Now create that vision for yourself. This is the easiest way out of pain.

We want our ex to be in as much pain as we are in. We lash out, and they respond with the same back. In the end, what was it for? It never satisfies and we end the relationship with bitterness, destroying any chance of a peace going forward.

Create a new habit when anger arises. Walk to the bathroom and look up to the right, towards the ceiling and ask yourself, "Is there another way of looking at this situation?" Then imagine a pale blue light of universal love flowing in and through every cell in your body. Allow the light to flow down your shoulders, hips and legs and drain all negativity out through the bottom of your feet. Now feel yourself connected to the wisdom of the universe.

In this new state ask, "Is this worth my energy and time?" "What am I presuming? What is my responsibility?"

There is only ever one person who can change, and that is you. If you change, everyone around you changes. How? Because your old self stops responding. You stop lashing out, you stop taking the bait, or creating the bait, you stop being passive. Who they knew you as no longer exists. When you change your response, they must change theirs.

You are amazing and intelligent; you are love. You release the past.

Releasing the ex

Release your ex. If you cannot wish them well, then at least wish them nothing, be neutral, especially if children are involved. You do not know what your ex came here to learn. You have no idea the karma they carry and the reasons why things happened the way they did.

Maybe the theme of your relationship was about learning to stand up for yourself. How many of your girlfriends would have put up with your ex? If your answer is one or none, then you have the lesson you came here to learn. If your girlfriends would have avoided your partner like the plague, then what did you need to learn by going through that relationship?

The universe is always looking to fulfil your dreams. But

if you keep focusing on your anger about the past, this causes your dominant manifesting vibration to drop. Like attracts like. How does the universe know what future you want? The universe does not have discernment. If you are not getting what you want, where is your attention? The universe only wants to fulfil your order. What is your order?

I focus on my highest path forward.

You will leave

If your boyfriend or partner is controlling, aggressive, abusive, manipulative, vindictive, has a substance addiction, is a narcissist, you will eventually get out. Whether you have children now, or whether you will in the future, you will (eventually) choose your children over your partner. You will realise it is not the environment to bring up children.

Having children amplifies differences. Any behaviour you found slightly annoying before children is catastrophic after children. Different parenting techniques are a cause of conflict. One parent might think smacking is okay and the other doesn't. Children rarely bring couples together. Sleepless nights, chronic tiredness, work stress, exhaustion put both parents on edge. Parenting tests your mental and emotional strength.

Decide that abuse of any sort is not welcome in your life. Choose the good guy; choose a loving father for your children. Mr kind, nice and respectful is out there. You just need to decide he is who you want.

I can choose the good guy.

Single parents

If you end up at some point in your life as a single parent, at no time should you permit a partner who is not the father of your children to discipline them. Be clear from the beginning: he does not touch or smack your children. Tell him you will not tolerate any mental, physical or emotional abuse towards your children. You will not tolerate bullying. You train/teach kids by your actions, not by your words; your partners are the same.

A man who respects you will hear your request and will admire you for speaking up and protecting your children. If he does not like your rules, or respect your word, then know his values do not match yours. Be happy not to have him in your life and know you have dodged a bullet. There is someone better out there.

Your partner teaches your children. He shows your son how to be a man and how to treat women. He shows your children how to treat you! He shows your daughter what kind of partner she should attract. He teaches your daughter how her partner should treat her.

Have you always said you wouldn't marry someone like your mother or father? You tie yourself to your children's father for 18 years. Think carefully. Do you want your boyfriend training your children how to be an adult? Do you want this man tied to your children forever?

> A prayer:
>
> If this relationship is not for my and my children's highest path forward, then please send your light to resolve this in the highest way for all concerned, so

all can move forward harmoniously with love, grace and ease.

Amen.

Short-term pleasure

Another tool to bring peace to your mind is to see where you may be using short-term pleasure to fuel your goals, to fuel your life and your relationship choices. Short-term pleasure can be munching on bags of chips or eating a block of chocolate when trying to lose five kilos, or when we spend our time watching TV or looking at social media when we know we should be doing something else.

Choosing short-term pleasure over long-term gain is okay when you do it occasionally. But when it is habit, you have a clue as to why you are repeating the past. Do you find yourself leaving some things until the last minute? Do you decide some things are too difficult and so why bother anyway?

One cause of choosing short-term pleasure is created by setting unrealistic goals. The sabotaging part of us knows we will never achieve them, and so we decide not to even try. We create destructive habits by making choices based on the easy option, the fast path, immediate pleasure. We think there is no one better out there for us, so we better keep him.

There isn't a too hard or a too long. There is just a start and a finish.

Should be doing

We always tell ourselves what we should be doing. We should be going to the gym, so we don't get fat. We should be eating our greens because they are good for us. We should be dating the good guy, but he's unexciting.

Why doesn't our should list work? It doesn't work because it is motivated by pain. Eating tasteless greens is painful. Calling ourselves fat is painful.

Running your life by a should list causes you to spend your life running away, avoiding pain. You sabotage your dreams, your health, and your relationships because your motivation to change is fuelled by pain, and we are always trying to avoid pain.

I release telling myself what I "should" be doing.

Motivated by extreme pain

Are you using extreme pain to motivate change in your life? If a lion was chasing you and caught you, you'd feel extreme pain. The lion serves its purpose, causing you to run fast to save your life. But using extreme pain does not work to obtain long-term permanent change. Extreme pain motivates us to change whilst the pain is immediate and intense.

Extreme pain likes one quick solution. Once the solution reduces the pain we revert to our old behaviour. This is why it does not work to solve your life problems.

If your life change strategy is motivated by extreme pain,

your pain will attract a guy who is resonating at that same level.

Our partners resonate with our motives.

Motivated by inspiration

Inspiration works as a motivator because it comes from a higher source and it feels great. It changes the difficult into the easy. Imagine how stress-free your school homework would have been if you had an inspired reason for doing it. If every time you opened your books or sat at your desk you thought, everyday I'm one-step closer to my goals, you would have a totally different outlook on your schoolwork.

Inspiration taps into love, which creates clarity. Love creates a peaceful mind, which allows the way forward to unfold. You then move swiftly, like a dart hitting its target, towards your goals.

I now see the hard path as just a path to start my way forward.

Positive motivation

Find a positive motivation for your goals. Instead of wanting to lose weight, choose to enjoy eating healthily or choose to get fit. Instead of fighting hate, support love. Instead of wanting to avoid bad relationships, choose to have a loving partner who respects you and who has the same values as you, etc. Focus on what you want, not on what you don't want.

Once you have your positive motivation, find the reasons behind your motivation, your "why". You must know your why. If your why is not big enough it will not inspire you to move forward through tough times. Your why is your driving force, keeping you inspired to follow your goals to manifest your dreams as reality.

Once you have your why, take it to its highest expression. For example:

"I'm motivated to eat healthily, to get fit, to have a clear mind, to keep my emotions stable, to be a better mum, to empower others, to make a difference, and to live each day with grace, uplifting all around me."

Each morning read your positive motivation, your why. Then visualise the day ahead, congruent with your why.

 Meditation: Clearing the past – Toy sack

Find a comfortable position on a chair or on the floor. Close your eyes and focus on the love of the universe. Imagine every tiny bit of air is filled with love smiling at you. Sit for a minute noticing that love is in the air all around you, smiling at you.

Now pretend that you have a Toy sack behind you, and that every negative belief you have ever held about yourself is going to pour into that toy sack. The beliefs move off the back of your head, your shoulders, beliefs such as, "I am not good enough, I am not enough, I must punish myself", etc. You might not even know what the beliefs are; you might just get a sense that they are peeling off you. Feel a lightness in yourself as the beliefs lift from you.

The Toy sack then transforms all within it, to love. And then releases that love to you and to our earth. You might sense that love as pink light flowing from the Toy sack.

Now imagine some happy times from the past. Whether it was seeing a baby smile, or cuddling a cat or a dog, or laughing with friends, your cousins, or anyone. Imagine seeing yourself as a gurgling baby, see that joy that you had, kicking your feet in the air, lying on your back on a blanket. It can be any moment where you felt joy.

Now imagine those happy times are like bubbles in the air, and those bubbles are filled with joy. Now notice that you are connected to those bubbles through golden cords. Notice that joy, love and laugher is flowing down through the golden chords and in and through you.

Know that those bubbles are your support team, they are always with you, and to feel them you only need to close your eyes and imagine the glistening bubbles connected to you, through the golden cords.

Now take a deep breath, wiggle your toes, open your eyes when you are ready and know that you are love.

 Meditation: Spark of life

Find a comfortable resting position, either on the floor or a chair.

Close your eyes and imagine a path in front of you. There is a gate up ahead. Imagine what colour it is and what it is made of. Open the gate and close it behind you. Continue on the path. There are flowers on the side of the path; smell or sense their fragrance. See the grass. There are birds chirping, flying in the sky.

Ahead is a circular staircase enfolded in walls made of light. Step onto the first step and continue up. With each step, you are becoming lighter. You see a rainbow above you. Whether you can see it or feel it, just know that it is there. Continue walking up through the rainbow. The staircase reflects the colours as you walk through them: red, continue up through the red light; orange, feel the courage, continue up; yellow, feel the clarity, keep walking up; green, feel the harmony; pale blue, feel your voice strengthening, continue up; indigo, sense your intuition sharpening; violet, feel wisdom enfold you.

Above the staircase you move into a beautiful white light. This is the light and love. Allow this light to flow in and through every cell in your body, through your mind, uplifting it to the realisation that we are all one. The air is filled with sparkling light and you feel at peace.

Your whole body is light. You are returned to your natural state: love and light. The spark of all life lies within us. From now on you remember you are love, you are light. You are love, you are light. Know that everyone in your life shares this spark. They all carry the light of love within them.

Ask your loved ones to come forward. See them come forward in a bubble of sparkling light. See the spark of light grow within them until they are bright light. Imagine their bodies are restored to complete health. See them smile with thanks and gratitude. Ask your loved ones to create a circle of love and light around you.

Feel their love flow in and through the cells of your body. Feel, sense, know that this light is restoring your body. Know that you can sense this circle and bring healing light in and through you and your loved ones at any time. Feel the love and gratitude flow to all in your circle.

Now think of someone you are having difficulty with. Imagine they are coming forward in a bubble of light into your circle, but they are without their earthly personality and come as their true self filled with their soul's love. Sparkling light has replaced any darkness within them.

From their true self they send love to you. You may wish to send them love or ask the beings of the universe to send them love on your behalf. Then see them in the bubble retreat into the distance, until the bubble is the tiniest speck of light and it is no longer visible.

See your circle of loved ones. Send them gratitude for being in your life. Receive their love and send them love. See your circle of light become more brilliant. See, sense, feel the light expand up, around and below your circle. See, sense, feel the love expand. You are one with the love and light of the universe.

See our Mother Earth come forward in a bubble of light. See the blue ocean, the green trees. See the bubble fill our home with love and light. See the spark of light appear as each person on earth is restored to light. See, feel, sense the joy from every person as they receive healing light. See the animal kingdom light appear. See love and healing light flow through every animal on the planet. Feel the love and gratitude flow from them to you. See the plant world spark of light shine more brightly now that your love fills their home. See our home planet earth filled with love. See the people on the earth laughing and smiling. See the spark of light within each human expand till every person is only visible as a brilliant star of light.

Feel the love and gratitude from Mother Earth. See our home expand with light. See the rivers and oceans flow with sparkling light. See Mother Earth within her bubble lift and retreat into the distance. See the bubble in the distance as a shining star of light.

See your circle of loved ones. See, feel and sense their radiant light. Send love and gratitude to them as their bubble of light retreats into the distance as beautiful stars. See behind you the rainbow of light.

See the violet light. Your staircase has appeared within the violet light. Walk to it and start down the staircase. Walk at the pace you enjoy down the staircase. As you step down and through the violet light, the staircase becomes filled with indigo light. Continue around and down through the pale blue light, then down through the green light, then down and through the yellow light, further down and around through the orange light, then continue down through the red light, until you step down and onto a patch of grass. Hear the sounds of birds.

There is a path in front of you. Follow the path down the slight decline. See the flowers along the path, take a deep breath and feel their scent. There are birds flying above. Hear their whistle as they fly past. See a gate up ahead. Open the gate and close the gate behind you.

Take a deep breath. Wriggle your toes. Move your fingers. Rotate your shoulders. Take another deep breath and slowly open your eyes. Have a drink of water. Look at the floor, look at your surroundings, have another drink of water. Enjoy. Know that you are love.

Highlights

- You distract yourself from your own life when you focus your attention on fixing someone else's.
- Each time you complain and speak with anger about your ex, your body is getting a dose of that hatred.
- The person you have been searching for is you.
- By finding success from suffering, victory from victimhood, you lay the seeds to thrive.
- Your partner teaches your children how to be adults.
- You are your children's and future children's protector.
- Using short-term pleasure as a short-cut to obtaining your goals ultimately sabotages your goals.
- Find a positive motivation for your goals.
- There is a future filled with love and joy waiting for you to show up.

❧ Reflections ❧

1. Create a wardrobe filled with clothing which reflects the person you will be in five years.
2. Look at your hairstyle and hair colour. Does either empower you to greatness? What changes can you make?

Daily practice – goals

1. Write down the positive motivations behind your goals and read them each day.

Imagine there is a pale blue light flowing in and through the top of your head. The light moves in and through you down and through your feet. Imagine there is a drain just beyond your feet and all tension and negativity are moving out the bottom of your feet and down the drain. Stay with this vision until you feel your body filled with pale blue light. Sit and enjoy the peace for a moment.

1. Take out your journal and write down a list of your goals and dreams.
2. Write a positive motivation for each goal and dream.
3. Take that motivation to its highest possible reality, for example, to create an earth where all humans, animals and nature live in harmony.
4. Enjoy the feeling, knowing that the highest expression for your motivation will benefit the world. Smile and enjoy your day!

Find a positive way to learn

1. What is this relationship or have past relationships been teaching you? Also add family and work situations.
2. How can you learn this in a positive way?

In this relationship, I'm being taught: e.g., *commitment.*

What is a positive way I can learn this? *When I start a project I now commit to finishing it.*

Moonlight affirmations

I allow myself to be victorious.
I am victorious.
I release living as a victim.
I allow myself to thrive.
I can thrive.
I can live each day thriving in my life.
I can live from my heart.
I can be in my heart.
I can radiate love.
I radiate love.
I can radiate love to all around me.
I can live my life without wishing ill on others.
I can live my life without anger.
I can release anger from my life.
I now live my life without resentment.
I release resentment from my life.
I can live without regret.
I can turn regret into a positive motivator to move forward.
I can be happy for others.
I can feel gratitude for others' good fortune.
I can celebrate their good fortune.
I can love myself.
I can accept myself fully.
I can value myself.
I am loveable just as I am.

CHAPTER 6

CHANGE

> "My grandmother wanted me to have an education, so she kept me out of school."
> — Margaret Mead

It is difficult to be a force for change when your mind is cloudy and your emotions have taken over. The right path never appears and fear of taking the wrong path becomes the motivating force.

I have found that one of the best ways to assist your mind to stop making up negative stories is to choose food which restores the mind to its wise self.

We eat to be healthy, to lose weight, to appear attractive, for comfort and in celebration. But very few of us eat for our brain health or our emotional health.

People who have spent many years or decades meditating will say they have gained a certain mastery over their mind. I have found some simple changes with food choices helped me with my mind and emotions. They may help you too towards attaining some mastery over your mind and emotions.

Your first steps

Whilst reading this chapter, look at your kitchen and how it is supporting you to manifest the life and the partner you have always dreamt of. Your kitchen needs to be a place of beauty, somewhere you enjoy being, creating food which you love which nourishes and heals you.

Look in your kitchen cupboards. What foods are you eating that still reflect the needy child? What snack and junk food from your childhood are you still buying? How many foods are there because your mindset says you deserve a treat? Who taught you that treats were food?

Instead of making food your treat, look to who can you treat with your presence. Do you have a grandparent who would love to hear your voice or see you?

When you are 80, will you look back with fondness at the box of sugary food? Or will you look back with fondness at the friends you've made, the places you've been, the people you have loved? How are you swapping food for loving the people around you?

Sugar

We love sugar. It is sweet, friendly, comforting and, above all, it makes our food taste great. Sugar exists in our food under a variety of names, from high-fructose corn syrup to synthetic sweeteners; fake sugar if you like. Some names for sugar on food labels are: fructose, glucose, agave nectar, honey, barley malt, beet sugar, brown rice syrup, rice malt, cane juice, etc.

Research studies have been conducted on sugar's effect on

the mind and anxiety. Sugar may be affecting your emotions, and one way you can find out if this is the case is by keeping a food diary.

If an issue wasn't bothering you, and now you are consumed by non-stop mind-looping, look in your diary over the past 24 hours to three days for the possible source. Take note, then next time your mind starts looping see if there is a pattern, that a certain food is triggering your suffering.

The ingredients list on packaged food is listed in order of highest to lowest amount. Take note of the top three to four items as they are what you are mostly eating. Serving sizes can vary. Check the nutrition panel and find the column which calculates the serving per 100 grams. Sometimes sugar quantity is listed according to teaspoons. Two teaspoons sounds better than ten grams. Labels are written in a way to play down their "bad" points and enhance the look of their "good" points.

It is your body. Know what you are putting into it.

Your diet can support you during this journey of change.

Kirsten

My friend Kirsten found that eating sugary foods set her mind off in continuous loops, causing her to swing from obsession to depression. She had thought her obsessive mind was just a part of her. Ever since she was a teenager, she analysed people's conversations, trying to determine the meaning behind their words. She suffered with anxiety and could never sit still.

After an illness, she changed her diet and removed all cakes and lollies, grains, except occasional rice, and eliminated packaged foods containing refined sugar. The unexpected side effect was that her anxiety symptoms decreased. She felt calm for the first time in her adult life.

Some weekends she would break her diet, which then flowed into the following week. It was during this time she met a guy. She began stalking him on social media. She found out where he lived, who his relatives were and how she could bump into him again.

When she returned to her diet of eliminating sugars she realised her obsessive nature was driven by the foods she ate.

Her natural state was not the anxious and obsessive person she had come to know herself as. She cleaned out her food cupboard and bought herself a book on what each food number on food packets means, and became her own food detective.

With her mind free of its old ways, she ditched the guy she was obsessing over and asked the universe, "Please organise a partner for my highest good." Previously, she could not do this; her mind would not allow her to step into the unknown. Her mind would not allow uncertainty into her life.

The universe responded and within weeks a new partner came into her life, just as she had ordered; someone for her highest good. Never in her wildest dreams did she think she would meet someone as gentle and sweet as he is. She said to me some months later, "For the first time in a long time I feel content and happy on the inside."

Simple changes

Change is tough when you rely on willpower alone. Disappointment sets in when results are slow. However, there are two simple changes which may propel you to eat healthily.

A few years ago, I discovered a short-cut that I now share with friends, family and work colleagues, who also swear by it. To reduce or stop altogether your craving for quick-fix food and sweet treats, add one teaspoon of apple cider vinegar to your water bottle daily. I have found that after seven days, a table full of desserts and sweets no longer has any control over me.

Look for apple cider vinegar containing the mother, preferably organic and in an opaque bottle. The mother is the cloudy formation at the bottom of the bottle. It contains raw enzymes and gut-friendly bacteria that promote healing. Always drink apple cider vinegar diluted in water. If you do not like the taste, add it to plain mineral water. This masks the taste and adds a slight flavour.

You can live without a limb, you can live without being able to walk, but when your mind is not your best friend, it's like living with an internal saboteur. Take care of your mind and choose your food wisely.

The power of our gut to influence our choices is often greater than our mind's ability to control those choices. Choose to eat for your gut health.

Your mind, your body

Instead of identifying as your mind, imagine you are your

body, listening to the mind's chatter. You notice that your mind's chatter is often negative, hurtful and spiteful.

In 2015, the Virginia School of Medicine announced that the brain has a direct connection to the immune system via newly found lymphatic vessels. The findings showed that your mind, immune system and gut are all linked. These unmapped lymphatic vessels were not in your doctors' textbooks or lectures.

The good news is that foods beneficial for your gut are now easy to find, whether at your supermarket or health food store. Foods such as kefir, a type of probiotic drink, homemade sauerkraut and probiotics. There are many gut health programs, books and functional medicine doctors specialising in healing your gut.

If we look at food as fuel, healing to our body and mind, we can choose foods that are beneficial for our mental and emotional heath. Foods which will assist us to achieve our goals to release the past and live an inspired life, filled with love.

Choose food which helps your mind to propel your goals.

Wheat and dairy

Some years ago, I developed an ear infection. It was my first and only one and I was in excruciating pain. When I recovered, I wanted to find a way to ensure I never went through that again.

I thought that the reason for my illness could lie in my diet, but I believed that I ate a healthy diet and didn't think there were any changes left to make. I looked to what functional medicine doctors were saying, which was that wheat, dairy and coffee could be behind a range of health problems. I couldn't cope with giving up coffee, so I chose to remove wheat and dairy.

We ate pasta weekly, so finding enjoyable replacements was a challenge. Over the years, I subjected my family to many alternative types of pasta, most of them ending up in the bin before dinner was over. I knew I had to find alternatives that were healing and delicious.

That's when I found rice wraps and rice pasta. This made the transition from pasta and bread easy. I bought rice milk or oat milk for our cereal. My children embraced the changes without even knowing it due to the range of palatable alternatives now available.

Sad

I noticed after giving up wheat that anytime I was feeling sad, I could always trace it back to eating wheat again. At work one day, we had sandwiches for the office lunch, as we were having a meeting. I chose what I thought were the healthiest, being the brown bread sandwiches. About an hour later, I dropped into an extreme sadness about a job I had turned down the previous day.

I walked around the office with my mind looping. I felt worried that I had made the wrong decision. After feeling bad for the next few hours, I asked myself an important question. Why wasn't this decision bothering me this morning or when I went to bed last night? Why am I feeling sad all of a sudden now? Was it what I ate for lunch?

The second that I had that thought, that maybe I wasn't the

cause of my sadness, I started to feel better. I went to the fridge and poured myself a drink of chlorophyll and water. Chlorophyll is what gives leafy greens and blue green algae their green colour. My chlorophyll was the only healthy drink I had at work and over the next 10 to 15 minutes, I continued to feel better.

That was the start of my awareness that food can impact your emotional state. I looked for research and found studies confirming a link between gluten and depression.

The food we eat can contribute to how we feel.

Further impact

My children and I all experienced different benefits from removing wheat and dairy. After six weeks, my children found their skin had cleared up, bad breath disappeared and dark circles under the eyes, which had been there for years, were gone. My daughter found her mind felt clearer and I found the congestion in my chest disappeared. We didn't anticipate any of these benefits when we gave up wheat and dairy.

Around this time, unbeknownst to me, two friends also gave up wheat. One found her stomach bloating cleared up, and the other's pattern of always falling asleep after the evening meal was gone! Since then, two more friends have given up wheat. Both travelled overseas after giving up wheat, and both said the same thing: that eating the bread in Europe and Asia did not cause them bloating.

Why wheat?

You might wonder why a food source that we have eaten for

millennia may be the cause of so many health problems. To find out why, we need to go back in history.

Our ancestors would not recognise our modern wheat. Some changes include crossbreeding and genetically modifying wheat to create extra yield. Research shows that the outcome of these changes is a reduction in mineral density. Governments in many countries have approved chemicals called herbicides (weed killer, i.e., glyphosate) to spray on wheat to dry it, nine days before harvest, a process known as desiccation.

The chemical interference with wheat continues when chemicals are used to age the wheat instead of letting it age naturally. Further intervention occurs with chemicals used to bleach the flour. After all this processing, some countries add a synthetic version of B9 to the flour, folic acid. Studies suggest that people with the MTHFR gene mutation, approximately 30 to 50% of the population, have difficulties absorbing folic acid, and therefore the real vitamin B9, folate may be more beneficial than the synthetic version. MTHFR gene mutation may be associated with heart disease, stroke, high blood pressure and, possibly, psychiatric disorders.

Our ancestors ate varieties of wheat such as emmer, einkorn and kamut. They soaked, sprouted and fermented their grains, which changes the grain and leads to many benefits. There are many books and websites devoted to the changes in wheat. Knowledge is power and we now have the power at our fingertips.

Health detective

We sometimes hear people say they would like to eat and drink what they like so they can die happy. But in reality food does not make them happy. The happiness of their loved ones makes them happy. By resetting how you view food, back to its purpose to fuel and heal your mind and body, you can be your own healthcare detective.

We hear a lot of conflicting information about what foods are good or bad for us. We don't know what to believe because what we were told was bad a few years ago, suddenly becomes good again.

When you hear about a new "health study", check out who is funding it. Confirm whether a PR company is promoting the study, and whether a particular industry benefits from it. Find out whether the funding is coming from entities with a vested interest. Investigate your local health associations, which tend to be the go-to experts. Ask yourself whether these associations can give an unbiased opinion.

Remember, a favourite attack is name-calling. When you hear corporations and people attacking with name-calling and negative slogans, ask yourself what is going on. Why do they need to resort to childish tactics to win their argument? What are they afraid of? Is there a deeper truth they are hiding?

It is your mind, your emotions and your body. You can be a food detective. You can make you your priority.

A clear mind

The greatest impact from changing my diet was the improvement in my mind, with clarity and sharpness and stable emotions. No more was I subjected to the emotional highs and lows that I found I lived with throughout my 20s and 30s.

I had become forgetful, but my sharp mind returned after adding bone broth to my diet. Bone broth is something that was made in our grandparents' or great-grandparents' generations and before. It was the basis of soups. Bones and vegetables simmered on the stove, beef bones usually for 48 hours and chicken bones for 24 hours.

Your healthy mind supports your inner change.

Mind and skin

Since starting the bone broth, I've also added raw garlic to my diet. Garlic is nature's powerhouse. I have found after consuming raw garlic I'm able to stay focused on my goals the following day. Somehow, eating raw garlic makes staying determined easy. Perhaps you will notice this too.

I use a potato peeler to create fine slices and scatter it over my dinner. This adds extra spice and improves flavour. I have also found the cleaner your diet is, the less noticeable garlic is on your breath.

I've found that nuts and seeds are small but powerful foods that help clear and hydrate my skin. You might like to try my sunflower seed and pepitas pudding mix, below.

I soak and ground the sunflower seeds and pepitas with a little vanilla essence, water and stevia and put the mixture in the blender, which makes a delicious pudding. Another delicious snack can be made by soaking cashews for four hours, then adding sea salt and roasting in the oven.

Scientific breakthroughs

Are you holding the belief that you cannot change because

it's in your genes? The epigenetics area of study is uncovering that we are not and have never been hostage to our genes; that diet, sleep and our emotional state are factors in the expression of our genes.

We are told as we get older that our health problems are just old age. But a quick internet search shows people in their 80s, 90s and beyond are still participating in body building, yoga, gymnastics and marathons, so if your body, mind and emotions are wearing out, how are you choosing to eat? Are you using food as fuel? What beliefs are controlling your food choices?

Breakthroughs in science are occurring constantly. We no longer have to wait for studies to filter down through governments into industry and into advertising. Keeping abreast of new information is easy. Many universities have an email signup page to gain access to their latest studies. Most scientific journals are available online and it is usually free to read the study's summary page which shows how the study was created and the results.

Not all fats

Our parents and grandparents in the 1970s and '80s were told to reduce fat in their diet to prevent obesity and heart disease. The food industry received this message and commenced manufacturing "low-fat" food, replacing fat in their processing with sugar and imitation sugar. But many scientists concluded that the research did not support the low-fat message.

The Framingham heart study of 1948, which ran for 20 years, showed lower natural cholesterol levels were associated with poorer performance on cognitive measures. Broda

Barnes published a book in 1976 called *Solved: The Riddle of Heart Attacks*. His book details the correlation between hypothyroidism and hardening of the arteries and heart attacks. In 2017, a study was published in *The Lancet*, which was conducted in 18 countries from five continents. Its findings included that high carbohydrate intake was associated with higher risk of total mortality, whereas total fat and individual types of fat were related to lower total mortality. The researchers concluded their findings by recommending that global dietary guidelines should be reconsidered.

We now know bad fats to be those such as trans fat, which involves a manufacturing process called hydrogenation that is used to turn healthy oils into solids to prevent them from becoming rancid in food processing.

Look into healthy fats such as avocados, flaxseed oil, chia seeds, organic butter, organic unrefined coconut oil, extra virgin olive oil, nuts, wild caught oily fish and free-range whole eggs. We have access to information and, as old and new studies show, we should consume good fats, which are beneficial for brain health and do not necessarily add to your waistline.

Sleep

It is difficult to make changes when we are sleep-deprived. I suffered with insomnia for around 16 years, which is why I started meditating, so that I could gain peace and remain calm through my sleep deprivation. Anyone who is sleep-deprived will know that anger becomes your go-to tool for resolving problems, thereby creating new problems.

A three-oil combination eventually broke my insomnia.

I started taking flax, fish and evening primrose oil to heal nerve damage caused by toxic levels of B6 my doctor discovered from my blood test. That combination of oils was a breakthrough for me in combatting insomnia in my life.

My doctor had not heard of using the oils for insomnia. I started looking for research linking the oils with sleep, but found none. I started reading the comments section in the purchases reviews and there I found that every fifth or six person mentioned that since taking evening primrose oil they were also sleeping better.

Juice recipe

The final solution to my insomnia problem was to make a daily green juice, which I find is better than a coffee to start the day alert and with a clear mind.

One of my morning juice recipes is: half an avocado, add in a green: silverbeet, cabbage, watercress, lettuce or baby spinach. Then add the juice of a lemon, a little natural stevia for sweetness, ginger, cinnamon and a green banana (low sugar).[1] Combine in a blender with some water or rice or almond milk.

Find what works best for you and create your own morning juice recipe.

Grow your own

Over the years, I slowly shifted to growing vegetables which required fewer pesticides, ones that the bugs seemed to like

---

[1] Thanks to my naturopath, Laura Wormington.

less. Having grown up around orchards and seen first-hand the amount of spray material used, I no longer wanted to eat food made this way.

Somehow, foods grown with pesticides became the norm in food production. I asked myself why would I want to eat my food dosed in chemicals and, more importantly, why would I want my children to eat food grown in chemicals?

Online you can find an old advertisement for DDT from the 1940s and '50s, promoting DDT as a safe pesticide. In the commercial, young people eat their lunch whilst sprayed with this chemical. DDT was banned in 1972 in the USA, but in Australia, the Government did not ban it until 1987. How long do you want to wait for your government to ban a toxic chemical?

I allow healthy food to nourish my body, my mind and my emotions.

Fresh food

Imagine walking through the fresh food section in the supermarket. On one side, you have a sign: pictures of fruit and vegetables with a skull-and-crossbones symbol. This picture is to alert you that this food is grown with pesticides and synthetic fertilisers.

On the other side is a sign which says "real fruit and vegetables". A leaflet tells you about the growers who nourish their plants with natural ingredients, who take care of the soil and the water table and our bees.

To enable supermarkets to create a point of difference to distinguish natural food from the pesticide and synthetic versions, a new section emerged: "certified organic". Depending on your age, back when your mother's or her mother's grandmother was a child, there was no need for an organic section in her local store. All fruit and vegetables were organic.

We now genetically modify our food. This is a new debate, which has generated worldwide protest. When spraying pesticides to kill weeds, certain genetically modified plants will not die. The research against GMOs (genetically modified organisms) is mounting.

I am not sure whether in 50 or 100 years' time the definition of insanity will include the race to "chemicalise" our food, our land, our water table, our people and our children. ("Chemicalise": a new word we should not need!)

I eat fresh food grown with love.

Get moving

As well as changing your diet, exercise is a great way to subdue your mind's chatter. Exercise can allow you to gain a new perspective on anything bothering you. Use your legs to get out and experience life. Athletes experience a high after exercise. I have experienced a high after a gym workout, and after a dancing class.

A friend recently walked the Kokoda Track and said she finally knew what a silent mind meant. Meditation is not the only way to experience inner peace. Walking can be a meditation when you use the time to be the observer. Exercise, yoga, jogging, bike riding or just stretching can bring relaxation to a busy mind. Painting, pottery, craft and gardening are all different forms of meditating and move you into your creative spirit.

Look at your surroundings. It is amazing to see the beauty that exists in our world, when the voice in our head allows us to be free to enjoy it. When our mind is silent, freedom is the result.

I take care of myself.

Remember, with any dietary changes, your tummy, your skin, as well as your gut instinct, are all used by your body to communicate with you. Consult with your doctor when making changes to your diet and healthcare regime.

Highlights

- In 2015, the Virginia School of Medicine announced that the brain has a direct connection to the immune system via newly found lymphatic vessels.
- Eat for your brain health.
- Eat to nourish your body.
- Eat to enhance your emotional wellbeing.
- Know when someone is targeting your fears to sell their product.
- Do not be a guinea pig for someone else's profits. Use discernment.
- Most scientific journals are available online and it is usually free to read the study's summary page which shows how the study was created and the results.
- It is your body; know the feedback it is giving you about the food you eat.
- Create your own garden to know where your food is coming from.
- Buy ethically as much as possible; our animal friends have died for us to live.
- Create a food journal or use an app.
- Check your pre-packaged food for "numbers".
  - Why are those "numbers" in your food?
  - Why do you need those "numbers" in your body?

❧ Reflections ❧

1. Create a kitchen of beauty, a place where you will love to be and cook.
2. Turn your kitchen cupboards into a haven of delicious, life-giving food.
3. Throw out, donate or re-purpose old pots, mismatched cups and glasses and create new matching sets that you love to use.
4. Clean, wash and use the bowls and dishes that you hide away for special occasions.
5. Check the food in your cupboards; how many items originated in a factory?
6. Look at the ingredients list on your pre-packaged food for numbers. How many "numbers" do you eat on a daily basis?
7. Shop at local farmers markets; get to know the people who grow your food.
8. Create a food diary. Each time your body gives you feedback, such as pain, bloating, sleepiness, brain fog, consult your food diary for what you've eaten in the previous 24 hours.

Daily practice

1. Listen to people you admire giving empowering speeches; they will uplift you and fuel you to follow your goals.
2. Try some of the easy changes below that you can make to your diet.

    - Fresh juices.
    - Add one teaspoon of apple cider vinegar to your water bottle (500 ml) once a day, for seven days.
    - Switch to organic milk, coffee and tea.
    - Create a vegetable garden (or pots) with vegetables which are easy to grow and do not require pesticides, for example, silverbeet, cucumber.

Important: Remember to check any dietary changes with a doctor or qualified healthcare professional.

Moonlight affirmations

I can create new habits easily for my highest path forward.
I can release old habits which no longer serve my highest path forward.
I can eat food that is nutritious for me.
I can enjoy food which is nutritious for me.
I enjoy eating fresh food.
I can enjoy cooking fresh food.
I now enjoy cooking fresh food.
I can learn how to eat food which is healthy for my body.
I can shop for fresh, healthy food.
I can cook fresh, healthy food.
I can enjoy eating fresh, healthy food.
I now thrive eating fresh, healthy food.
I thrive eating fresh, healthy food.
I am joy.
I am love.

CHAPTER 7

ACCELERATE

> "The purpose of our lives is to give birth
> to the best which is within us."
> — Marianne Williamson

Congratulations, you are on your final chapter of change. This chapter is here to assist you to evolve into your highest life. From here, you manifest the future, the partner, the love, the life you have been longing for.

In previous chapters we have looked at how your little self has been running your life, with its petty disputes, its petty grievances, its petty disturbances, but who you are is greater than all those things. Now is your time to step up and live the life you've dreamt of, and leave your past behind.

You are an amazing, magnificent person, the owner of your life, the driver of your story and you can create it the way you want it. With focus, attention and a passion for renewal, you have the power and the love to stand up and embody your highest life, and call in a life partner, boyfriend or husband who matches that higher life, who loves and respects you for being you.

Your first steps

To support the new you and your manifesting a loving relationship with a partner who respects and uplifts you, take a look at your friends, family and work colleagues. Who amongst the people you see regularly inspires you to lead a life of joy, health and love? Who in your life supports and uplifts you?

Is there someone in your circle of friends who backstabs and gossips? Your friends can be your greatest enemies, keeping you stuck in a mindset of pain, repeating the past.

Make a decision to give up gossiping, and only say uplifting things about others. Excuse yourself when the conversation turns to attacking others.

Ask the universe to bring in new friends who empower and uplift you. Join a gym, yoga or pilates class or find a running or exercise partner. It is hard to gossip and exercise at the same time. People who exercise are more likely to have a mindset of self-improvement.

Allow those friends who disempower you, who want to keep you stuck in the past to drift away. Those people are on their own path to enlightenment; their path no longer needs to be your path.

The life you've dreamt of, the partner you've dreamt of, the joy you've dreamt of all exist from the small daily changes you make. Small insignificant changes are part of a huge movement towards love, peace and joy in your life.

Who am I?

Are you kind, nice or both? Who do you think you are? At your core, which one are you? Have you struggled sometimes to say no? Do you find social occasions difficult? Knowing whether you are nice or kind has a bigger impact on your life than you would think.

Just let the questions repeat across your mind several times: "Who am I? ... Who am I exactly?" I asked myself this question one night whilst driving home from the movies, when it hit me: I am kind, but I am not nice. I wondered how I could hold such a belief, and then I remembered that I learnt from a very young age that I had to be nice in order to be "a good little girl" – the praise for being nice – otherwise I was "a bad girl".

The problem with conditioning girls to be "good little girls" is that we grow up and filter every decision we make through the mindset: "Am I being nice?"

If every time you said no you were scolded for being "a bad girl", then as an adult, you may feel you have violated some inner code each time you want to say no. The fear of not being nice kicks in and you say yes when you want to say no.

But a person who grows up believing they are nice does not have a problem saying no, because they do not filter their response through the thought, "But what if they think I'm not being nice?" They know themselves to be nice, and so the fear of being "not nice" does not occur to them.

Teach your daughters to be loving, caring, ethical, kind and to have values. Teach them how to say no when their values are violated, but do not label them nice, not nice, good or bad little girls.

I attract in a partner who reflects my highest values.

Own best friend

Are you your own best friend or are you your own worst enemy? I have seen over the years that successful people are their own best friend. Your worst enemy does not live outside of you.

To determine whether you are treating yourself as your best friend or worst enemy, check in with your internal dialogue. How do you speak to yourself? Are you attacking? Do you put yourself down for making a mistake?

Remind yourself, you are amazing. Look where you are now, how far you have come. In ten years' time your future self will be pleased you embarked on this journey. Give yourself praise for moving forward, for taking steps to move up to your higher life, your greater loving self who has the power to change the world.

I am amazing. I am my own best friend. I can change the world. My voice matters.

I got you

A Course in Miracles, by Helen Schucman, says that the ego, or your lower mind, is "capable of suspiciousness at best and viciousness at worst". One technique to release the mind's grip on you is to tell it to "stand down". Your mind needs to know you are in control, that you've got this. Otherwise, it will repeat itself like a nagging parent.

We are used to our mind telling us what we can't do. Have you ever realised how down you can feel after listening to your mind's negative chatter? But when if your mind tells you, "you've got this", how great it can feel?

Choose from this moment onwards to be your own best friend. Choose that your internal dialogue will be like a sports coach. It will be supportive and give you a pep talk when things don't turn out as you planned.

You will be amazed at how good it feels to have your own mind tell you, you can do it. Your internal coach can drag you off the couch, out of bed or over to the desk, or wherever you need to be, with just a few uplifting words such as "come on, you can do it".

Try it. Tell yourself, "I can do this" next time you encounter a challenge and you will see how much better you feel.

Be your own coach. Tell yourself, "I can do this."

Reframe

If your childhood pattern was to give up at the first setback, you might be used to your mind saying something like, "Oh, you were stupid to think you could do this." Reframe what you think is failure. Allow your inner coach to take over.

Ask yourself what you are learning here. Realise that failure is just feedback. Some of us were brought up to believe that failure was the end, failure is bad; but instead of that, it's just showing us a new way forward, or that we need to engage resilience. When failure steps into your life, reframe it. Ask an empowered question, such as: what is the best way forward?

Failure no longer limits me. I always ask: what is my best way forward?

Memories exercise

Think back to your earliest memory of giving up, then think of another memory, and then find a third memory if you can. As you find each memory, ask yourself what you decided in that moment – what did you make true for yourself that is now causing you to repeat the past?

Now create a new picture of the past where you did not take that path, where you did not make that belief. Then vision yourself in the future as a person who moves past obstacles, who finds new opportunities out of failure.

I know nothing

I have learnt the path to wisdom, and happiness, is through asking better questions. Asking questions teaches us to stop interpreting events with the lower mind, which is where viciousness and suspiciousness can often manifest. When we challenge our thoughts, we cease to be battered by the voice in our head.

One day my daughter ran out of the house and jumped in her car. She was upset; her ex-boyfriend had called her. I knew she was not in any state to drive, and that she should not confront her ex at any cost. I also knew that a "mother's speech" was not going to make her get out of the car and stay home.

Whilst asking her what happened, I silently said the prayer, "Please help me, I do not know what to say, please give me the right words for her highest path forward." I started speaking and within a few seconds, I found myself saying the right words, and my daughter returned inside.

I allow guidance into my life.

Intuition

Your gut instinct – or your intuition – is your guide in this lifetime. Some people know where they are going and what they are doing, others have no idea. They ask their friends for advice, they do courses, read books, but they can never shake their indecisiveness. Intuition is your guide out of indecisiveness.

For some, intuition is an image which flashes across their mind's eye; for others, it's a feeling or a knowing. We are all different and we receive our intuitive hits in different ways. Listen in to every feeling or twitch your body has – you are getting a message. Have you often thought, I knew I shouldn't have done that. Your intuition gently guides you towards the best path, but your conscious mind often overrides it.

The best way to develop your intuition is to honour it when it appears. When you get that first feeling or hunch that you should do something differently, follow it. Practise on small things at first until you learn to trust it. Your intuition is like a muscle – the more you use it, the more you will understand when it is hinting at you to choose another path.

Your intuition is a small feeling inside; it is not something that is yelling at you. Your mind is loud, so you will need to cultivate the practice of turning within. A sense of profound peace and joy can be found within these inner states. And the practice will allow you to know when your gut instinct calls you to follow a new path forward.

Ensure you don't walk around holding your breath. Breathe and tune in to your body's messages at every opportunity.

However your intuition comes to you, honour and nurture it, and your confidence will grow, and you will know when to take action when an intuitive hit occurs.

Be open to a higher wisdom guiding you to your life partner, boyfriend, husband.

The request

One day, my mind was tormenting me. It was looping with the reasons why a particular person should apologise to me for the pain and destruction they caused in my life. I knew receiving the apology was impossible, but my mind would not stop. I found myself becoming more wound up with anger by the second. I didn't like that feeling, and I desperately wanted my peaceful mind to return.

I had read once that we can ask for problems to be "lifted" from us. In desperation I asked: "Please lift this from me. I cannot resolve it. Please help me release this situation, and resolve it within me for everyone's highest life and help me move forward without this."

My relief was instantaneous. My mind stopped its loop immediately. I was astounded by the sudden silence. Then I felt the relief and joy to have my peaceful mind back.

My request to the universe for help was a passionate plea from my heart. Whether you call it a prayer, a request, a pleading to the universe, to a higher energy, to God, it must be a heartfelt request. I've found a mental request for help does not work as powerfully.

Ask the universe for help.

Gratitude

Gratitude can build a pathway out of pain. Many years ago, after breaking up with my boyfriend, my mind, body and emotions went into shock. It was as if our past together did not exist. One day he was here, the next he was gone.

Focusing the mind on loss causes the heart to be flooded with sadness. That sadness then seeps through our entire being. Our mind then attempts to justify the heart's torture with its never-ending loop analysing every aspect of, what went wrong, who's guilty and finally, what's wrong with me? Ultimately, the mind only searches for pain.

I knew that thinking about the loss. Thoughts such as I've lost my best friend, I miss him, I'll never love again – caused me pain. And I was not going to allow my mind to keep me stuck in pain. Pain feels bad, and I choose not to live there.

If we use pain as a signal to change our thoughts, we can find the pathway back to joy. When I thought about the wonderful times we had, I felt happy. When I thought about the bookcase he fixed, the tiling we did together, the outings with our kids, my sorrow disappeared. Gratitude for the little things brought me back to my loving self, my happy self.

Gratitude opens the heart to love, which relieves the mind of its burden to find a justification for sadness.

My friends said to me, "I can't believe how well you've handled this breakup." I told them gratitude was my tool. It is what released me from pain's grip. Our emotions follow our minds thoughts. Our hearts will break if we allow our mind to be our guide with lower, negative thoughts. Pain is the result, and pain is our clue that we are thinking something that does not serve our highest good. We are thinking something that will block us manifesting our highest life. Be the owner of your mind. Do not allow your mind to own you.

I allow gratitude to release me from pain and return me to love.

Meditation: Change your state

We can easily shift into fear. When you do, remind yourself you are love. Sit or lie down. Breathe in and count 1-2-3-4, breath out, 1-2-3-4. Find your own relaxed breathing rhythm.

Remind yourself: "I am love. I am light. I am love. I am light."

Imagine your heart as a ball of pink light expanding. Feel the warmth of the pink light fill your body. Follow the light, breathe and remind yourself: "I am love. I am that I am."

Follow the pink light, allow it to expand to fill the room you are in. Expand to fill your house, the building you are in. Expand to fill your suburb, fill your state. Imagine everyone who is touched by this pink light immediately feels it and feels light; their entire being is calming down.

Feel the light expand to your country and then to fill the entire world. See the lakes and rivers healing with this light. See the animal kingdom healing. See our trees receiving nourishment. See our oceans healing with this light.

See the pink light of love fill the heart of every woman, man and child on this earth. See the pink light of love within every person shining brightly, expanding to fill their entire being.

Pray for peace, pray for love to fill our earth, pray for healing for all beings on this planet. Pray for love to be humanity's highest value and guiding light.

Open your eyes, smile and have a wonderful day.

Be love

I've read many books that said the same thing: we must love ourselves. I have done affirmations in the mirror such as "I love you, you are lovable". I have put positive affirmations inside my closet door, but I felt I was tricking myself. I still felt empty when I didn't have a partner to reassure me I was loved.

My three-year-old son taught me what love is. Every night I would sit on his bed and we would list the people who loved him. One night, as he reached the end of his list, he said, "And I love me." From that moment, I knew he would have a happy life, that he would never search for people to love him. Loving yourself creates a vibration that attracts friends and partners who have the same vibration at their core.

When we look for love and approval from others, we destine ourselves to disappointment. We tie our happiness to someone else's version of reality. Our joy rests on their values and we fail to ask ourselves if their values are congruent with ours. When our core value is love, our approval is all we need.

My highest value is love. I attract in a partner based on my highest values.

The revelation

I had a revelation when our family cat, Shadow, died. At the time I was single. Shadow had started sleeping on my bed each night, snuggled behind my back. Shadow was friendly when she wanted to be, but she could take a swipe at you if you patted her too much. I was the privileged one in the house to have her sleeping with me. I decided that if I did not have a partner, at least I had her.

That is, until I awoke one morning to find she had passed away on our kitchen floor. I had resigned myself to being a happy cat lady and not even that was meant to be. I was back in bed alone once again.

When I thought about how I had lost her and she was gone forever, I hurt. When I thought about her sitting up at the ceiling, shining her love down on me, I felt great. It was such a contrast. When I thought about how much I loved her, I felt love.

I thought about my other losses, my grandmother and my father. When I thought about their loss, I felt pain. But when I thought about how much I loved them, I felt great. The thought that they are alive, just not visible, but up above, sending their love to me made me feel love.

When we give love we feel love.

I am love

We do not need to love ourselves; just be love. This is our

true nature. The love we have been searching for all our life resides within us. We have been seeking our true self our entire life.

Just for a moment, think of a baby smiling up at you, with its little feet and hands moving with delight. It is sending you love. Giving and receiving love is where our bliss lies. When you no longer need someone to provide you with love, you are free.

When you radiate love and joy, your loving vibration helps others to lift, to rise to love also. Have you ever walked into a room and felt the atmosphere, and known something bad has just happened? Or have you ever been in the presence of someone who lights up the room when they walk in? Have you ever locked eyes with someone across a room, and known that they are feeling what you are feeling?

That is energy, and you feel it every day without realising it. Every time you drop your energy to the lower vibrations of hate and anger, you send that vibration out like a ripple across the universe, and those vibrations are picked up by others; maybe by someone about to commit a crime. Just imagine that from now on you only send love across the universe, and what kind of world we would live in if we all did the same.

Be love and radiate love to all beings on our planet, all animal life, and know yourself as love, and that the only reason you feel pain is that you have stopped loving, whether someone or a beloved animal.

The person you have been searching for is yourself. There is no one to chase or find once you remember who you are. You are a magnet for higher vibrational people. There is only your equal to meet, that person who resonates with that same love as you do.

I am love and I attract in a partner who resonates with love.

⁓ Meditation: Your true nature ⁓

Find a comfortable sitting position, whether the floor or a chair. Close your eyes and relax, and calmly, rhythmically breathe. Breathe in, 1-2-3-4, breathe out, 1-2-3-4. Relax down into your chair and breathe to the number beat that suits you. Make it the same in and out relaxed, calm, even breath.

Imagine someone you admire. Imagine their qualities. They might be confident, bold, intelligent, resilient, charismatic, loving, enlightened, wise ...

Breathe and feel them sending you these qualities. Feel them enter your body and permeate every cell from your toes to your head and all throughout your aura.

Know yourself as love. Feel the energy of being love. You are love, you are light.

Know yourself as enlightened. Feel that state. Your higher self knows that state; allow it to fill you now.

Imagine yourself filled with all these new qualities standing in a doorway, looking at a room filled with people talking and laughing.

How would you stand as your new self? What thoughts would you think as your new self? How do you move as your new self?

Walk into the room smiling. See people noticing you and smiling back, saying hello.

How do you speak as your new self? How do you laugh as your new self?

Allow these qualities to integrate through your entire being. This is you, your true nature, your highest state.

Open your eyes, smile and have a great day.

Be love exercise

Start a relaxed, even breathing pattern. Feel how your feet connect with the floor. Sense the top of your head and feel how it connects to a loving universe. Sense the universe smiling down on you. Imagine the sun is smiling down upon you.

Imagine that every cell in your body has just turned 45 degrees upwards to receive the love and joy from the universe. Feel the love flooding your cells, as each cell jumps for joy as you allow the love and light of the universe to flow in.

Receive the love and joy from the loving, wise beings around the planet who emanate love. Feel the love from your ancestors, from the animal kingdom, from nature. Just sit and feel for one minute all the love that exists around you. When you are ready, slowly open your eyes and smile. ☺

Higher purpose

Our higher purpose is what we all unknowingly crave. We crave to contribute, to be of service, but many of us do not recognise it. If you are feeling down and you have not thought about how you can contribute and make a difference in this world, then you have a clue to how you can move out of pain.

Have a look around at the young celebrities and sports people. The ones who are thriving are the ones who give back. They realise that working in their dream job, earning their dream money isn't enough. True joy comes from making a difference, finding meaning and purpose.

Find somewhere that you love being, where you are at total peace, whether that is the shower or a walk in nature. At these times, ask yourself what is your higher purpose. Repeat the question over and over without expecting an answer. Just let the question wash over you whilst you focus on what you are doing, and see what answer you receive from the stillness of just being in the moment, enjoying where you are.

Another way to find your purpose is to post this question on your desk and bathroom mirror: "In 12 months' time, what will I wish I had done today?"[1] For myself, I would answer this question with "finish my book".

These small life purpose reminders move us in a direction that brings us easy transformation. It does not work magically over night, but day after day, your reminder sets in motion the path to easy change, change that lifts your life to daily joy.

The universe gives us a new sun every day. No two days are the same. Magic happens when I ask: "Please guide me. Who should I speak to? What should I say? How can I be

---

1   Liam Linisong.

of service?"[2] Whether at work or at home, I find amazing conversations start by being open to something greater. The universe never fails me when I ask to be of service.

I have a purpose here on this earth. I can attract in a partner who is on the same path as me.

Karma

In any situation, our response is our power. Our actions affect our karma. Other people's actions and choices affect their karma. If you view karma as a bank account, one account contains your positive balance, the other your negative balance. You want to keep your account with the positive balance higher. Allowing annoyance to deplete your account is nonsensical. Attacking with anger and revenge depletes your reserves. You do not need the depletion that attacking thoughts bring.

I walked out to my car one day to see a scratch on my rear passenger door. I immediately thought their karma will sort them out. The energy of that thought gripped me around my ribs. That thought dropped me into a self-serving smugness, delighting in the karma that might befall the perpetrator.

I knew it wasn't my business, and that thought, along with the feeling of smugness that it was their karma, was not making me feel good. Feeling that smugness wasn't the same as feeling unconditional love, bliss and joy, and I did not want it there.

I asked myself how I attracted this incident. Was it something I had been thinking? Or had I just been saved

---

[2] Inspired by *A Course in Miracles*.

from something worse, a car accident perhaps? These questions removed me from the other person's business and put me back into my own business, into what was my responsibility.

As soon as I asked these questions, I no longer cared about how or what had happened to my car, or who or what the perpetrator was. I had freed myself from my thoughts, and the scratch served only as a reminder that the past wasn't the future I wanted to create. I felt free and I felt blissful that I was now creating a wonderful future for myself, one that didn't include repeating negative events from the past.

It is sometimes easier to see the play of karma in other people's lives. Watch the celebrity roundabout – karmic examples abound. Look at all events as potential karmic builders or karmic drains.

I see my good karma all around me.

Release

As your karma moves into balance, the period between negative event and negative karma shrinks. If I ever allow myself to drop into anger, it will only be a few days before I see someone return the anger to me. We normally notice negative karma and register it in our brains, forgetting that karma is not judgemental. We call it good or bad, but it's just cause and effect.

We can release ourselves from the play of karma. Karma only occurs in response to what we hold within us. On the lower levels of the earth plane where anger, hatred and revenge exist, so does the play of karma. As you evolve your consciousness, you leave karma behind by uplifting your dominant state to love.

Like attracts like. As you become lighter you attract in a partner made of the same loving vibration as you.

The I am

One day I was doing an exercise with my life coach. We had been jumping up and down and yelling, just some of the weird and wonderful exercises he had me do on occasion. I sat back down in my chair, and out of nowhere, unconsciously I said, "I am that I am." My coach was astounded. He said to me: "Do you know what you just said?"

This revelation of the "I am" state cemented me in the knowledge that we are love and that we are light. We have nothing to strive for, just the unfoldment of love and service amongst our fellow beings; acting in a way that brings light to all beings on this planet.

Radiate love whether it's to someone in the light, in heaven or a thousand miles away. Feel that your heart is open and receiving the love that permeates our universe.

I choose to attract in a partner who radiates love and joy.

Our highest state

People ask me how I maintain my calm state. The reason I am calm is that I know my highest state – love. Calmness and peace are the effect of knowing my highest state.

If I ask you to get out your journal and answer the question, "Who are you?", most people will respond with: "I don't know, I'm human, I'm a girl, a woman", etc. All are true, but who are you at your core?

Joy is one of the highest states, next to love. When we know ourselves as love or joy, we know who we are. We are the embodiment of our divine potential.

Our higher states of love and joy are where peace and harmony live in our lives. Once you have love or joy as your highest state, as your core, you will have all of the states around it: joy, peace, happiness, calmness, right-mindedness, and your wise mind as your guide.

If you live in your highest state, when a challenge arises you still may drop down into anger, but you won't stay there for long and will soon move back into your wise mind.

Once you shift into love and joy as your normal state, you want for no one and nothing. You are content with your life. This does not mean that you do not want a loving partner, or stop aspiring to see the world living in peace. It just means you do not need someone or something to make you happy. You are happy. Love is where creativity, drive and passion live. It is where your higher purpose, your higher calling lives, your destiny in this world.

I attract in a partner who matches my highest state.

Future self

Ask yourself, what do you need to do to have the best partner possible? You do not need an answer straightaway. Once you ask the question, your subconscious will work on the answer.

You may meet someone who might trigger some new thought

process within you, or you might get a hit of inspiration to take a new course of action.

Now is the time to step up and be the person you have always wanted to be. Maybe you have let doubt or shyness block you being the next Oprah, the next Malala Yousafzai or the next J.K. Rowling. Vision yourself as your future self, until your future self becomes second nature to you.

I step into my life as my future self. A partner who matches with my future self is waiting for me.

Meditation: Future self

Find a comfortable sitting position, whether the floor or a chair. Close your eyes and relax, and calmly, rhythmically breathe. Breathe in and count 1-2-3-4, breathe out, 1-2-3-4. Relax down into your chair and breathe to the number beat that suits you. Make it the same in and out relaxed, calm, even breath.

Imagine yourself five years in the future. What is your highest future? Let your imagination go wild. Who could you be? Who do you want to be? See yourself as that person.

Where are you? What are you doing? Are you a leader? Do you inspire people? What is your highest possible future? Your future self – see her, feel her, and take in the surroundings. What is she doing? How does she do it? How does she walk? How does she greet people? How does she talk? How does she love? How does she express her confidence? How does she laugh?

Sit for a minute and watch her, your future self. Now merge yourself into your future self. Imagine that you and she are one. Bring her fully into you. Bring in her lessons, her wisdom, her confidence, her charisma, her authentic self, her authentic voice, etc.

> What other qualities does she bring to you? Feel her and know yourself to be her. Sit for a moment in your new energy. Know yourself as her. You are one.
>
> Repeat as often as needed to stay in alignment with your future self.

Brilliant

We all have our own love and wisdom within us. Shine and be your own light.

Allow yourself to follow your passion, to show up and shine.

Oprah Winfrey said that everyone who came on her show asked this one question when the interview was over: "Was that okay?"[3] We all hold the same insecurities within us. Sometimes the only difference between you and someone you admire is that they did not give up. Allow yourself to follow your passion, to show up and shine.

I allow myself to shine. I attract in a partner who matches my vibration.

Morning exercise

Start each day connected to gratitude. As soon as you wake up in the morning, connect with the energy of gratitude. Think of things that make you grateful. It may be your child laughing; it may be your childhood pet; it may be a sunset. Connect with the vision of something you love. Feel it, see it, remember the sounds, recall the fragrance, the colours. Now turn up the colours, the sounds, the fragrances and

---

3   "An evening with Oprah", Melbourne, 2015.

make them more vibrant. Make them as real to you as if you were there right now.

Think about everything that you are grateful for, no matter how big or small. It could be for the fresh clean air, a smile you received yesterday, the job you see yourself having in the future, your new partner. Be grateful for what you have in your life, what you may have in the future. Imagine you have all of those things now.

Then vision for yourself the type of day you would like to have. You can choose to vision the day, the week or the year ahead.

Morning prayer

Universe, please guide me. Who should I speak to today? What should I say? How may I be of service? Amen.[4]

---

4   Inspired by *A Course in Miracles*.

Highlights

- Being conditioned to be "good little girls" means you say yes when you want to say no.
- Cancel the thought, "What if they think I'm not nice?"
- Remind your mind: "I hear your concerns." Write your mind's ramblings down in your journal.
- Your intuition is your own inner guide in this lifetime.
- Allow yourself time to be with your inner self. Breathe and enjoy the glorious being that you are.
- Ask yourself wise questions: "What is my next right step forward?"[5]
- Gratitude releases you from the pain your mind can create. Your feelings follow your mind's thoughts. Be vigilant when your mind takes you down the path of negativity.
- Gratitude also moves your energy into a higher vibration, the vibration where manifesting lives.
- Karma is just cause and effect. Every action creates a force within the universe, be that negative or positive.
- Acknowledge positive karma, acknowledge good fortune, and be thankful for it.
- You are love.

---

[5] Acknowledgement to Oprah Winfrey.

~ Reflections ~

Contemplate

1. How often do you find yourself gossiping?
2. Who in your friendship group brings you down, or loves to keep you stuck?
3. If someone is gossiping to you, then they will be gossiping about you when you are gone. Make a decision to only say things which will empower and uplift another person.
4. Visualise your friends inspiring and uplifting you, laughing and creating experiences together which empower your group.
5. Align with your highest state each morning.

The checklist: Moving forward

Close your eyes. Take some deep, relaxing, calming breaths. Imagine that you are connected to the wisdom of the universe through gold cords which lift up into the heart of the universe, then open your eyes and write in your journal.

1. Who are you at your core?
2. What is your highest future?
3. What is calling you?
4. Where do you want to live?
5. How can you create your highest life?
6. What is your next right step forward?[6]

---

[6] Acknowledgement to Oprah Winfrey.

Moonlight affirmations

I can be my own best friend.
I can trust myself as my own best friend.
I can trust my intuition.
I can sense my intuition.
I know it is safe to trust my intuition.
I trust my intuition.
I can feel my gut instinct.
I can sense my gut instinct.
I can use my gut instinct to guide me.
I can be grateful for my life.
I can live my life with gratitude.
I can live my life from my highest path forward.
I can believe in myself.
I can live my life believing in myself.
I believe in myself.
I can make good choices.
I can safely say no.
I can choose to say no.
I can live my life being love.
I can be love.
I am love.
I can be love and radiate love to all around me.
I can speak from love.
I can be grounded and speak with love.
I can be grounded.
I allow divine order in my life.
I allow my divine destiny to unfold.

End of Part 2

You can choose to remember your past as transforming you into the magnificent being you are now. Know that you can now live in the light and amazing glory of your true self, your authentic self, fuelled by joy, enfolded with love.

Know that a relationship based on love, peace and joy is your divine right, and that you now accept your divine right.

It is your time to shine!

PART THREE

CHAPTER 8

MANIFESTING

"If music be the food of love, play on."
— Shakespeare

Welcome to your final chapter, where you call forward your soul mate and life partner. Our power to manifest lies in our ability to be centred in our heart, aligned with our desire and our highest state, the vibration of love. Your dominant vibration acts like a magnet sending out a call to that which is like you.

Soulmates and life partners

We believe that we need to manifest a soulmate, but soulmates do not always make great romantic partners. As soulmates, you might talk about how you are two sides of a coin. All may seem great at the start, but then you notice that your soulmate pushes your buttons, challenges your beliefs and challenges your motives. If you are ready to move forward at a cracking pace, releasing beliefs, practising forgiveness of self and others and love of self and others, then this may be the perfect relationship for you.

An alternative is a relationship with your life partner. In some ways, this partner can be too perfect. You drift along spending most of your time on the couch, out to restaurants, living one day after the next. If that sounds great, then add it to your manifesting list. But sometimes with nothing to challenge you and no way to move forward, life can be just one day after another.

If you are feeling stuck in your current relationship or past relationships, ask yourself, what did you give up on? Where did you allow your creative self to be hidden? What dreams and desires did you give up? What did you decide was just too hard to achieve? What possible future is calling to you now?

I can step up into my higher calling.

Be authentic

A key to a relationship is not just meeting a person you are happy to spend time with, but meeting each other's authentic self. A friendship is where you do not need to show up as someone else, where you get to feel safe being yourself.

One of the best ways to manifest a new life partner and soulmate based on and connected with your authentic self is to move in the direction of your life purpose.

Allow yourself to step up into that grander self, that grander life that you know has been calling you.

I allow my authentic self, my highest vibration to guide my life.

Purpose

Sometimes when we are not connected with our purpose,

we can drift from relationship to relationship, job to job, never feeling completely fulfilled in life. We then seek our purpose through jobs we hate and unhealthy relationships. We can feel lost in this world.

Shifting our focus to the question, "How can I serve?"[1] connects us with our life purpose. Synchronistic opportunities flow our way and we connect and resonate with friends and family at a higher level.

Think of gossip and attacking conversations as low-level conversations, generated by our small self. When we ask, each day, "How can I serve?", we naturally drift away from engaging in lower level conversations. When we move into our life purpose, our friends will lift with us, or new ones will find their way in.

Ask how can you contribute to making the world ONE, where all people can live in harmony, joy and peace. When enough people focus on this question, we will create a world where this is a reality. We often live our lives as if we are alone. However, none of us can exist without each other. What we do matters; the changes we make to serve a higher good impact all humankind and our animal and plant kingdom.

When you align with your highest path, magic happens, doors open. Every positive change you make, your family receives the benefit. If you have children you will see them growing and blossoming every time you make a change. It's not what you say to them, it's what they pick up from the changes in you. Your life partner/soulmate is waiting for you to step up into that grander life.

---

1   Oprah Winfrey, "An evening with Oprah", Melbourne, 2015.

I can attract in a partner who holds my values of serving the highest good of humanity.

Stepping stone

Sometimes when we commence manifesting a new partner, other steps need to happen first. Do not be disappointed if your next relationship ends. See every occurrence as a stepping stone leading you to your ultimate relationship.

The universe cannot violate your free will, if what you want is in conflict with what you are tolerating, i.e., allowing people to treat you in ways you would never treat them because you are not setting your boundaries.

The "no longer tolerate list"

Decide what you will no longer tolerate in a new relationship. Start a list of everything that you will not accept. Stand in your power, knowing that you are on the road to consciously creating your life. Affirm your list to the moonlight.

Burn or tear up your "no longer tolerate" list. Burn it in the fireplace or other safe location, or destroy it in whatever way feels right to you.

Say to yourself: "I no longer allow people to treat me this way. I do not treat myself this way. I now allow in positive, uplifting people as friends, work colleagues and romantic relationships. I now allow in people who love me and respect me, and who uplift me to be a better version of myself."

Your next relationship might be the stepping stone to the one you desire. Ask yourself what you need to complete or what project you need to start to bring forward your life partner/soulmate. Often you will know the answer as it is something you have been procrastinating about.

Sometimes we need to change course after getting what we wanted, realising it didn't make us happy. This is why meditation and aligning with your highest state each day allows you to more easily make life's course corrections, the feather duster approach. The sun rises each day and you get to choose again, whether you course correct or stay on your current path.

There is always someone better.

Relationship goals

If you don't have a relationship goal, now is the time to be clear on the type of relationship you want. Think of an aunty, uncle or friends that are in a long-term happy marriage. If you do not know anyone, look for a happy, stable, long-term celebrity marriage.

Create a list of relationship goals and values, and at the top write which ideal couple you aspire your life to be like. Create a vision for yourself inspired by their happy marriage.

New relationship

Being on the constant lookout for a new partner moves your energy out of the present and into the future. You no longer live your life with certainty. Thoughts like, "maybe I'll meet someone at this event, or at this nightclub, surely I'll meet someone tonight, I'll swipe yes to this guy, maybe he will be the one ...". These thoughts hijack your life. When you stop needing someone, the right person who will lift you to the next level will show up.

Release yourself from looking and keep your focus on how you want your life to be. Move your thoughts into certainty. The past is gone. The future just needs your consciousness in the here and now to create it.

A wonderful guy will appear in a perfect way in accordance with my divine timing.

Your list

Consider the following for your manifesting list.

- Date an equal, not someone whom you consider smarter or better than you, or someone you will look up to. Date an equal and you will feel listened to, that your views are valid, and you both contribute to the relationship.

- Ask for someone who shares your values, who shares your lifestyle goals, your vision for the future. Someone who values communication and has mutual respect as one of their values.

- Ask for someone who is compassionate and empathetic, who understands there are two sides to every situation, who understands forgiveness and is able to forgive.

- Ask for someone who accepts you as you are, who respects your authentic self.

- Request the best person for you to come in. Don't sell yourself short by asking for someone who is "at least better than the last one". That is not your life anymore. You are stepping up to your new life, and with that stepping up comes a better man.

- Ask for someone who wants to grow with you, who wants to be the best version of themselves.

- Ask for stability, that is, someone who is mentally, emotionally and financially stable. Someone who knows how to handle a bad day.

- Ask for someone who understands how to be responsible.

- If you are dating online ask for normal. You are meeting people whom your intuition would filter out if you met them in person, so asking for "normal" is one way to filter out those that you would automatically filter out in person.

- Ask for someone who is compatible. You do not need someone to have the exact same interests and hobbies, but someone who has views and an outlook on life that are compatible with yours.

- Ask for someone in a similar life circumstance. It is not essential, but if you have small children or older children consider someone in a similar circumstance, or if you have no children someone without children. They will understand your situation and are more likely to be on the same page as you.

- Ask for a partner who compliments you. Allow the universe to bring forward your highest relationship, the relationship which will lead to your greatest peace, love and fulfilment on this earth.

- Ask that you love and get along with his family and his family loves and gets along with you, because you marry the family!

Consider the following for your manifesting list.

- Monogamous
- Faithful
- Loving
- Attractive to me
- Gets along with my family
- I get along with his family
- Compassionate
- Shows his love
- Respects me as I respect him
- Empathetic to others
- Loving communicator
- Honest
- Loyal
- Trustworthy
- Values in alignment with mine
- Generous
- Kind
- Dependable
- Stable
- Open-minded
- Financially stable
- Emotionally stable
- Committed
- Life purpose compatible with mine
- Fun
- Joyous
- Sexually compatible
- Loves to laugh
- Warmth of character
- Happy disposition
- Beliefs compatible with mine
- Single and available (you don't want to manifest a married man)

Include the physical attributes you desire.

Manifesting boyfriend/partner

Prayer: Please bring me into alignment with my highest next divine boyfriend/partner. Someone who respects and loves me (and loves and respects my children). These qualities (list them) or better for mine (and my children's) highest good in accordance with my divine path.

When you go to bed at night, just before you fall asleep visualise yourself with your new boyfriend/partner according to your list, having fun with you, speaking respectfully, etc. Engage all of your senses (see senses exercise below).

I release the past. I now allow in the love and support of the universe to create a future filled with love and joy. I allow in a loving life partner/soulmate.

Senses exercise

To enhance your relationship manifesting and connect with a higher vision for your life, you need to be able to engage all of your senses.[2] To engage all of the senses we are going to switch them on and enliven them, ready for manifesting. Do this exercise often.

For a moment, imagine these tastes:
Eating your favourite chips: salt and vinegar/chicken/BBQ, etc.
Sucking the juice out of a lemon
Licking the cream or topping off your favourite cake

Just for a moment, imagine feeling:
Your hands plunged into a bucket of cold water

---
[2] Acknowledging Jean Houston, Quantum Powers training.

Jumping into a cool swimming pool
Reaching your hands into a bag of potato chips and crunching them with your hands

Just for a moment, imagine hearing:
The waves crashing onto the beach
A lion roaring
A car revving its engine

Just for a moment, imagine seeing:
A sunset
A cat or dog playing in the backyard
Your favourite cartoon

Just for a moment, imagine smelling:
The fragrance of a rose
Your favourite perfume or cologne
A cake just baked

Prayer for manifesting a new romantic partner

Before starting the prayer, centre yourself in your heart. Tell yourself you wish to move into alignment. Feel the love all around you which permeates our universe.

Ask your angels, guides or someone in the spirit world to come forward to lift your vibration and to assist with your manifesting. Sit and attune to their energy for a minute. Feel the love and support of all the beings in the universe.

Dear Universe, please send your light to enfold me with your love, so that I may know my true self. (Wait, sit, feel the energy.)

Please send my love to all beings who live on this planet.

Thank you for releasing my beliefs which keep me stuck, creating the disharmonious thoughts against my brothers and sisters. (Wait, sit, feel the energy shift.)

Please send your light from my soul to the soul of my compatible life partner and soulmate according to this list, or someone better, for my highest good.

Thank you for bringing us together in alignment with our highest path and with divine timing.

May all humanity live in love, peace and harmony. Amen.

Keep your eyes closed and watch as the light from your souls meets and converges into a large silver-white star. Breathe and sit in the energy of your prayer.

Little book of manifesting

An amazing manifesting tool is what I call the little book of manifesting. Buy yourself a small notebook that will fit in your handbag or that you can keep beside your bed. Your little book is where you will write your manifesting list for the preceding seven days.

Before starting, lift your vibration by thinking of all the things you are grateful for in your life. Close your eyes and imagine it is next week already. Imagine all the things that have happened in the past seven days that you are grateful for.

Then write the date at the top of the page, not today's date, but one week into the future. Start your writing with "Thank you for ...". Choose three things: a personal quality, an event and a personal aspect.

- A personal quality is something you would like more of in your life, such as determination, perseverance, intuition, enlightenment, joyfulness, etc.

- A life event you would like to manifest in the future might be a loving life partner and soulmate based on authentic love, or a workplace where you are respected, etc.

- A personal aspect might be gratitude for your healthy body, fit and athletic. Always include this or something better and for your highest good and in alignment with your divine timing, and if you have children, add in for their highest good.

Then as you go to sleep, visualise what you have written using your senses to see, feel, taste, hear and touch your manifesting, accepting that these things have already happened, feeling the joy that this is your life. If you are grateful for meeting your new partner, see that vision, picture it in detail, feel the joy.

I release my list to the universe to bring this or someone better for my highest good and according to my divine timing.

Little book of manifesting example

Date: Seven days in the future

Thank you for my life partner and soulmate, who is aligned with my values, who is compatible with my life purpose, who is my equal, who I'm attracted to, who I'm compatible with, who loves, respects and adores me and loves and respects my children, someone who is stable[3]. This or

---

[3] Acknowledging Vianna Stibal.

someone better for my (and my children's) highest good and in alignment with my divine right.[4] Thank you.

We want what is ours to flow to us with grace and ease by our divine right, not something or someone taken from another.

Meditation: Calling in a like-minded romantic partner

We find it easier to connect with someone who is like us, someone who has the same values as us. There is nothing more satisfying than holding a conversation with a like-minded friend. They hear everything you say and you are both interested in hearing each other.

Find a comfortable sitting position, whether the floor or a chair. Close your eyes and relax, and calmly, rhythmically breathe. Breathe in and count, 1-2-3-4, breathe out and count, 1-2-3-4. Just relax down into your chair and breathe, counting the number rhythm which suits you. A relaxed, calm, even breath.

Imagine there is a beam of light from the sun streaming in through your home. It is the love and the light from around the sun; allow this light to flow in and through you. It contains all love and all wisdom.

Allow the light to flow in through the top of your head, down through your head, face and through your neck. This light is flowing down through your shoulders, soothing them and releasing the muscles. You can ask for your troubles to be lifted from you and sent to the light to be resolved in the highest way for you and your loved ones, allowing the consequences of any wrong decisions to be undone for everyone's highest good.

---

4   The concept of "divine right" is discussed in Florence Scovel Shinn, *The Game of Life and How to Play It*.

Allow the light to continue moving through you, down through your chest and arms, in through your digestion, down to your hips, through to the top of your thighs. Moving the love and light of the sun down to your knees, your calf muscles, your ankles and out through the bottom of your feet.

Sit for a moment in the healing light of our sun.

Call in a like-minded romantic partner who is on the same wavelength as you, someone who has the same values, someone who is compatible with your life purpose, someone who will become your best friend, someone whose values are love and joy ... (from your manifesting list).

Ask for this person, or someone better, someone who is in alignment with your highest life (and for your children's) and in alignment with your divine right.

Send your message up to the light of our sun. See the light from our sun shine down on your new romantic partner, for your and his highest path forward.

Watch as a spark of light shines up from your new romantic partner to form a star in the night sky as both of your souls meet. See a large, shining silver-white star holding the light of new beginnings.

Sit in this love for a moment. Take a deep breath in, have a drink of water, smile and have a great day.

Vision board

A vision board is a great way to see your new future. For those who are not visual by nature, the vision board gives them the ability to visualise easily. The vision board gives your imagination a head start. Cut out images of what you want to manifest. Pin up pictures of loving couples, the type of family unit you want to create, the type of house and atmosphere you want to live in.

You can create a vision book instead of a vision board. Get creative. Whatever suits you best. Not everyone who has used a vision board has looked at it daily. I know someone who bought the house from her vision book that she packed away several years before buying the house.

Remember when looking at your vision board or book, lift your vibration and feel the love and joy, as you picture your new life inspired by the pictures on your vision board or book.

Morning exercise with life purpose

Each morning before you get up, visualise what your future looks like. Shift into a gratitude state by focusing on all that you are grateful for. Then visualise the future as if it was real right now. See yourself laughing and talking with your new partner and holding hands.

Now visualise your life purpose or how you would like to be of service. See yourself loving life and fulfilling this purpose. See the people impacted, see their joy, know that you have moved into your life purpose. See your life partner/soulmate supporting you on this journey.

Manifesting notes

Ripple

Everything you say and think is sent like a ripple across

the universe. Nothing is without consequence. When you break your word you send contradictory messages about your manifesting to the universe.

How often do you break your word? You say you are going to exercise and eat better, give up soft drink, smoking and coffee, but a few weeks later you've thrown in the towel and gone back to old habits.

Reflect on your past. How many things have you given up on? Where did you break your word to yourself? Ask yourself often, what do you need to know to manifest your dreams? Take baby steps at keeping your word.

Do not say anything you do not intend doing or following up on. One small act each day turns into something larger over 12 months. Soon your word will be your honour, your bond with yourself and the universe, and your life won't be held hostage to the saboteur inside.

Break the habit of breaking your word, it is delaying your manifesting.

My words matter; they create my universe. I now speak and think for my highest life path and for the highest life path of those around me.

Vibrational state exercise

Eliminate lower vibrational conversations with friends and work colleagues as these drop you out of your highest state. But if you do drop your vibrational state you can reset yourself back to your highest manifesting state by doing the following exercise.

Imagine the cells in your body are like receptors waiting to receive love and each cell is smiling out towards the world as well as inwards towards you. Imagine people around the world, like lights, all vibrating love. Their love sends out a ripple which enfolds the entire earth. All you have to do to receive that love is to ask it to, "come on in".

Take a calming breath and gently close your eyes. See every cell in your body smiling. Now see/imagine all the ripples of love flowing across the world. The air is filled with love.

Meditation

Now see/feel/imagine the cells in your body are absorbing love from those ripples. Sit in this state and feel yourself uplift with love and peace.

The love within you now magnifies and sends out its own ripple, joining with the sea of love surrounding the earth. Your love now expands and multiplies as it ripples around the world , sending a healing vibration of love, peace and harmony around our world.

Your love vibration is your signal to the world around you, and to the partner you are manifesting. Keep your vibration high by being love. Align yourself with love and allow in your highest possible romantic partner.

I allow in a partner who matches my highest vibration.

Manifesting thrives

To continue your manifesting take notice of how much

relaxed breath you take in. Have you ever noticed that you feel anxious or ill at ease when you shallow-breathe? A relaxed state will connect you back into your highest state, where you remember to connect with love.

We often deprive our self of water, replacing it with caffeine and sugary drinks. How much clean water do you drink each day? Is it reasonable to expect your mind, body and emotions to thrive if most of what you drink is sugar and caffeine-infused?

Your most important assets are your mind and emotions. Check in each day and remind yourself to allow in the basics of this life: air and water. Don't allow a lack thereof to pull you out of your highest state.

Be in alignment with love, and peace will enfold you. The mind will calm and your body will follow, allowing you to stay aligned with your highest state and manifesting your romantic partner.

Manifesting thrives when you can maintain your highest state, which is love.

Timing

After completing this chapter know that the universe is working on your request. Move forward with creating your life's purpose and you will see the universe does answer your prayers, often in ways better than you could have ever imagined.

If you suddenly feel down for no reason, check in and ask yourself what you ate in the last two hours, which may have triggered this sudden change. Food may not have been a the cause, but if you don't allow yourself to observe you will never know.

Ask for grace to enfold you each night before you go to bed. Shine the light of that grace out into tomorrow and next week, through into next year, so that the path you walk is filled with grace – the light and love of the Divine.

Joy

Love and joy are contagious. Just smile for three minutes in the mirror and see if you can feel bad at the end of it. Feeling great is where we want to keep our energy; it is where synchronistic events live and it is how we quicken our manifesting.

A smile can change someone's day. We know not what good a small smile can bring to others' lives. The compassion of a stranger, a smile from a colleague. Together, we can create the change that the world desperately needs.

It starts with you, right now, to live within your larger self and leave the little self behind. Your little self is concerned with petty grievances, living out a small existence. We all have a mission and life purpose. A grander life was mapped out for you before you came here.

Everything you have survived in this lifetime is a testament to your strength and ability to pull through the toughest of times. This has built within you a resilience that you can build on.

You are here to be someone in this world. Whatever your career, whether it is grand, important or ordinary in your eyes, you have no idea what your contribution to the lives of others is. You do not know who you were meant to intersect with in this lifetime, or how your words or deeds may change others' lives. To live a life of purpose, attune each day to joy. Maintain your manifesting energy by aligning with joy.

My birthright is joy. I am joy. I attract all that is joy to me.

Manifesting consciousness

Enlightenment

We can create peace. It starts with one person at a time evolving their consciousness. That means lifting yourself out of the cycle of fear. Many years ago, in certain circles, it was frowned upon if you said you wanted to be enlightened. But now Yogis are teaching that it's our birthright and it is our goal for this lifetime. We do not need to know how or which way is the path to enlightenment. All we need to do is to set enlightenment as our goal.

I have found anytime I am in meditation and I ask the universe to teach me what it feels like to be enlightened, I feel the most amazing peace come over me. If I say the affirmation, "I am enlightened", I can feel the energy, and often find amazing synchronicities and wisdom come from conversations after aligning myself to this energy.

I manifest a new relationship with love.

Two-minute meditation: I am love, I am light

A quick pick-me-up you can use at your desk or when visiting the bathroom is to close your eyes and relax, and calmly, rhythmically breathe. Breathe in, 1-2-3-4, breathe out, 1-2-3-4. Relax down into your chair and breathe to the number beat that suits you. Make it the same in and out relaxed, calm, even breath.

Remind yourself: "I am love, I am light, I am love, I am light." Imagine the love of the universe permeating, healing and reviving the cells of your body. Then, whilst you go about your day, repeat the mantra to yourself: "I am love, I am light. Allow me to feel what enlightenment feels like."

Open your eyes, smile and enjoy your day.

The Divine

There is a greater peace, which comes from connecting to a higher wisdom. Life choices are clearer and you feel a greater sense of stability through making these decisions with a higher source.

The human experience in its grandest composition offers learning unlike any other. Our life, captive within the flesh, twists and contorts, struggling to find meaning and purpose within the confines of its straitjacket, the body. The body has an inbuilt antennae system to receive signals and process them. Signals which are ignored and unprocessed lead to decay and disharmony within your life.

Violence fuelled by anger is the lowest form of justice in the human experience. We don't realise the cause and effect which is set up by their use. If you knew there was no escape from anything that you did, would you think twice before taking action?

Genuine soul love is the highest form of justice in the human experience. Allow grace to flow in and through your life every moment of the day. Ask for grace to resolve the injustice you see in the world. Ask grace to resolve the issues in your life. Pray and ask for the light to intervene and resolve for everyone's highest path in this lifetime.

You are love. You are grace. You are harmony.

Attuning to light

New beginnings abound when you attune to the loving force of the universe. We release ourselves from the mind's projection of the future. Faith, trust and strength appear with the knowledge that we create our reality. Allowing yourself to drop into fear and negativity draws more of those negative emotions to you.

Allowing the Divine in to guide your life is not rescinding control, but is moving in alignment with the loving force of the universe. Grace, if you like, means to move into alignment with your highest good, your highest potential in this lifetime. You never lose control, because you never had control; your control is over your reactions.

When you release your personality, your ego, from calling the shots, your true self, your divine self has the opportunity to bring your goals and desires into reality. By aligning with your divine self you walk the earth path with assurance. Your gut instinct and intuition are your connection to your divine self. Nothing comes at the expense of someone else.

Our lower self may decide this or that event is bad, but we do not have the same vantage point as our angels. Things happen; it is up to us to find meanings from those events which empower us to move towards love, not away from it.

I allow in a partner who aligns with the divine within me.

Wise self

Many have lost connection to the universal life force. It is the energy that weaves through all things. The reason for our existence often haunts us and the decisions we make. Questions we wonder about, but do not often ask aloud. What is the meaning of life? Why is there struggle? Why is there pain?

Losing the connection with our divine self leaves these questions unanswered and life without meaning.

The mystics and philosophers of old felt this guiding connection and left us detailed information. Permeating throughout spiritual texts and philosophers' writings is the guiding force of the universe. We are not alone, and have never been. Our aloneness comes from separating ourselves from this universal life force, the Divine.

We are love.

Connection

As you move into knowing, you understand that the universe does have your back. Humanity's happiness is its will. We often fear the Divine and the will of the Divine taught through various teachers and traditions. We think that if we trust the Divine we will lose someone or something that we love. We think that to lose something or someone is divine will. We think that we have a God who uses human justice, human logic of good, evil and punishment. This is simply not true; the Divine, or All that is, or God has no desire to take anything from you. Do you not think that God has everything already?

Everything you do and say is creating. Lightness and love are a way of being, not something you do only on holy ground. Understand that the whole earth is holy. This brings you back to correct consciousness. Every moment is holy. Every animal on this earth is holy. Everything you do is seen and it is holy. Create love, be love.

When you live life at this level you no longer need to chase your dreams. Your dreams walk into your life. You take the steps. You follow your intuition. People show up at the right time. Good men abound and there is no lack, as you no longer resonate at the level of lack. Your life partner/soulmate by your divine right is out there waiting to meet you.

I am the love of the universe. I am divine. I am love. I allow in my life partner/soulmate who resonates with the highest aspects of my loving self.

You can create your life fuelled by love, enfolded in joy and powered by your divine right. You are part of an earth story that evolved over eons, created from love.

CONCLUSION

The five signs and nine filtering patterns are your tools to break the patterns created by attracting in partners who have been resonating with your lower aspects. Your old patterns of resentment, anger, bitterness no longer need to attract in your romantic partners. Those past relationships were teaching you how to release these lower aspects from control over you, how to return to love.

Your life circumstance has been drawing in the perfect opportunities to help you make the shift to living an empowered life.

As you break down the barriers inside you which have kept you away from love, you release the hold the past has had on you. As you step into your new vibration, you release a force out into the universe, creating a new energy of attraction, bringing to you, your new romantic relationships based on your highest vibration, which is love.

Your shift changes your vibration and allows in a soulmate or life partner who resonates with those higher aspects within you.

You are the one you have been searching for. Your loving self is who you have been longing to meet. It is the authentic you, the joyous, loving you. Know that love that lives within you. You no longer need to chase love.

You can allow the universe to draw in a romantic partner who matches with that which you are: love.

When your consciousness uplifts to love, you can create the life that has been waiting for you. You then set up the energy that connects you with other like-minded people. You can attract in the romantic life partner/soulmate you have been yearning for.

Your life partner/soulmate is waiting to meet you.

We live in a world where for the first time in human history the survival of our species is at stake. Playing the game of life at this low level is leading us all to pain.

Our mission here on this earth is to uplift, and as you uplift your energy it creates a ripple which enables others to uplift, and thus stand in their power, one with each other, one with love.

We are all One, connected by our real Self which is love.

This is the golden age.

This is the age of love.

CONCLUSION

Highlights

- There is no "one" that we need to find. You are the one you have been searching for. There is a romantic partner waiting to meet the authentic you.

- Love ripples across the world; allow your cells to receive it and feel uplifted. This love will send out an echo to call in your romantic life partner/soulmate.

- By lifting your vibration daily, aligning with your highest state, you move into the energy of manifestation.

- Align your values with the highest values of the universe, being love, joy, courage, etc.

- Focus on your goals which support your greater good, as well as the greater good of those around you.

- When something negative appears in your life, ask a better question. What is this teaching me? What was my responsibility?

- What is the best way forward?

- Life repeats, asking us to make new choices that support our highest self. Your inner wise self is waiting to assist you. Let yourself in. Let love in.

- Life is happening for us, helping us to break free from our lifelong habits.

- We are co-creators in this lifetime.

- Peace starts in the home within the family unit. We can contribute to uplifting the world, one person at a time.

- Know we are love. You are love. You are loved.

- Know that the universe is conspiring in your favour.
- When wonderful coincidences happen, acknowledge them and say thank you.
- When we live each day in our highest state, we never feel alone and the mind returns to its true purpose, being a tool for the body, there to create life consciously, manifest your dreams, inspire creativity.
- Choose alignment, choose joy, choose love, choose grace.
- Attune daily, lift your vibration up to grace and see your life unfold to joy and make manifesting a joy.
- Every moment is a moment to choose love over fear, to release pain.
- Connect to the wisdom of the universe daily.

I create my life with the loving support of the universe.

CONCLUSION

❧ Reflections ❧

1. What do you need to complete or what project do you need to start to bring forward your life partner and soulmate?
2. What greater vision of your life is waiting to break forth?
3. What small steps can you take on a daily basis to live in alignment with your highest life path?
4. Ask the question daily, "How can I serve?"
5. Daily prayer: Thank you for showing me the path to my highest life, the path of love, light, to my joy.
6. Choose to no longer judge events as either good or bad. Instead ask: "What are you teaching me here? What do I need to know? How can I learn this lesson easily with grace and ease?"
7. There is a future waiting for you to show up, there is a life partner/soulmate who matches your new vibration.

Journal moment

Write down your relationship goals.

What wisdom can be gained from today's events?

How would you like tomorrow to unfold? What dream is trying to manifest in your life?

If you could be anything in five years' time what would it be?

Moonlight affirmations

I now have a loving relationship with a man/life partner/soulmate who is my equal.
I now attract in a boyfriend/partner who is an equal.
I now have a loving relationship with a guy/soul mate/life partner who has the same values as me.
I allow in a loving, respectful relationship.
I allow myself to connect with my life partner/soulmate in accordance with my highest path and with divine will.
I can meet my life partner/soulmate in accordance with my divine right.
I can live, love and be respected as my authentic self.
I know my authentic self.
I feel safe being my authentic self.
I live from my authentic self.
I can trust divine timing and my divine right.
I can live my life in alignment with my divine timing.
I can live my life as my divine self.
I am divine.
I can be brilliant.
I am brilliant.
I can live my life with joy.
I am joy.
I can radiate joy.
I have a life purpose.
I can step into my life purpose.
I can allow the universe to reveal my life purpose.
I am love, I am light.

CONCLUSION

Reminder

- Each morning wake and remind yourself: "I am love." Align your day with love.
- Your dominant vibration attracts in life circumstances that match your vibration.
- Manifesting your dreams by aligning with your highest state.
- Meditate daily, whether it's a walking meditation, or a meditation whilst gardening, jogging or doing yoga.
- Find your time to connect to the universe/divine/highest state.
- Ask empowering questions.
- Seek solutions.
- Choose your food based on how it will nourish your mind and emotions.
- Visualise your future self.
- Follow the morning routine.
- Create a vision board or vision book.
- Say the morning prayer: "Please guide me. Who should I speak to today? What should I say? How may I be of service? Amen."
- Live an enlightened life.
- Be love, be light.
- Change the world!

FURTHER READING

Helen Schucman and William Thetford, *A Course in Miracles*

Maya Angelou, *Still I Rise* (poem)

Florence Scovel Shinn, *The Game of Life and How to Play It*

Gerald Jampolsky, *Love Is Letting Go of Fear*

Don Miguel Ruiz, *The Four Agreements: A Practical Guide to Personal Freedom*

Marianne Williamson, *The Gift of Change: Spiritual Guidance for Living Your Best Life*

Gabrielle Bernstein, *The Universe Has Your Back: Transform Fear to Faith*

Caroline Myss, *Entering the Castle: An Inner Path to God and Your Soul*

Byron Katie with Michael Katz, *I Need Your Love – Is That True?*

Eckhart Tolle, *A New Earth: Create a Better Life*

Elizabeth Gilbert, *Big Magic: Creative Living Beyond Fear*

Sanaya Roman, *Living with Joy*

Viktor E. Frankl, *Man's Search for Meaning*

Vianna Stibal, *Advanced Theta Healing®: Harnessing the Power of All That Is*

Anything by: Dr Jean Houston, Marianne Williamson, Oprah Winfrey & Caroline Myss

BIBLIOGRAPHY

Agrawal, Rahul and Fernando Gomez-Pinilla. "'Metabolic syndrome' in the brain: deficiency in omega-3 fatty acid exacerbates dysfunctions in insulin receptor signalling and cognition", *The Journal of Physiology*, vol. 590, no. 10, 2012, pp. 2485-2499. Accessed 18 December 2016, <onlinelibrary.wiley.com/doi/10.1113/jphysiol.2012.230078/abstract>.

Australian Government Department of Health, "Personality disorders", n.d. Accessed 13 March 2017, <www.mindhealthconnect.org.au/narcissistic-personality-disorder-npd#!>.

Bahl, Rahul. "The evidence base for fat guidelines: a balanced diet", *Open Heart*, vol. 2, no. 1, n.d. Accessed 11 December 2016, <openheart.bmj.com/content/2/1/e000229>.

Carlson, Linda. "Mindfulness-based cancer recovery and supportive-expressive therapy maintain telomere length relative to controls in distressed breast cancer survivors", *Cancer*, vol. 121, no. 3, 2017, pp. 476-484. Accessed 2 September 2017, <onlinelibrary.wiley.com/doi/10.1002/cncr.29063/full>.

Dehghan, Mahshid, et al. "Associations of fats and carbohydrate intake with cardiovascular disease and mortality in 18 countries from five continents (PURE): a prospective cohort study", *The Lancet*, vol. 390, no. 10107, 2017, pp. 2050-2062. Accessed 31 December 2017, <www.thelancet.com/journals/lancet/article/PIIS0140-6736(17)32252-3/fulltext>.

Elias P., et al. "Serum cholesterol and cognitive performance in the Framingham Heart Study", *Psychosomatic Medicine*, vol. 67, no. 1, pp. 24-30, 2005. Accessed 11 December 2016, <www.ncbi.nlm.nih.gov/pubmed/15673620>.

Fan M., et al. "Evidence of decreasing mineral density in wheat grain over the last 160 years", *Journal of Trace Elements in Medicine and Biology*, vol. 22, no. 4, pp. 315-324, 2008. Accessed 28 December 2016, <www.ncbi.nlm.nih.gov/pubmed/19013359>.

Gilbert, E. *"Big Magic"* Bloomsbury Publishing Plc, 2015.

Guerrero Schimpf, Marlise, et al. "Neonatal exposure to a glyphosate based herbicide alters the development of the rat uterus", *Toxicology*, vol. 376, 2016, pp. 2-14. Accessed 28 December 2016, <www.sciencedirect.com/science/article/pii/S0300483X16300932>.

Harcombe, Zoë, et al. "Evidence from randomised controlled trials did not support the introduction of dietary fat guidelines in 1977 and 1983: a systematic review and meta-analysis", *Open Heart*, vol. 2, no. 1, 2014. Accessed 5 March 2017, <openheart.bmj.com/content/2/1/e000196>.

Huang Y, et al. "Maternal high folic acid supplement promotes glucose intolerance and insulin resistance in male mouse offspring fed a high-fat diet", *International Journal of Molecular Sciences*, vol. 15, no. 4, 2014, pp. 6298-6313. Accessed December 2016, <www.ncbi.nlm.nih.gov/pubmed/24736781>.

Ibrahim M. and E. Okasha. "Effect of genetically modified corn on the jejunal mucosa of adult male albino rat", *Experimental and Toxicologic Pathology*, vol. 68, no. 10, 2016, pp. 579-588. Accessed 18 December 2016, <www.ncbi.nlm.nih.gov/pubmed/27769625>.

Jess, Allison. "DDT environmental effects", ABC Goulburn Murray, 11 October 2007. Accessed 11 December 2016, <www.abc.net.au/local/stories/2007/10/09/2054547.htm>.

Kharrazian, Datis. "Your brain on sugar", Why Isn't My Brain Working?, 2013. Accessed 18 October 2016, <http://brainhealthbook.com/brain-sugar>.

Koehler P., et al. "Changes of folates, dietary fiber, and proteins in wheat as affected by germination", *Journal of Agricultural and*

Food Chemistry, vol. 55, no. 12, 2007, pp. 4678-4683. Accessed 11 December 2016, <www.ncbi.nlm.nih.gov/pubmed/17497874>.

Li Wang, et al. "Effect of a moderate fat diet with and without avocados on lipoprotein particle number, size and subclasses in overweight and obese adults: a randomized, controlled trial", *Journal of the American Heart Association*, vol. 4, no. 1, 2015. Accessed 10 December 2016, <jaha.ahajournals.org/content/4/1/e001355>.

Louveau Antoine, et al. "Structural and functional features of central nervous system lymphatic vessels, *Nature: International Journal of Science*, vol. 523, 16 July 2015, pp. 337-341. Accessed December 2016, <www.nature.com/articles/nature14432>.

Mercola, Dr. "Scientists find direct link between brain and immune system", Take Control of Your Health, 25 June 2015. Accessed 16 October 2016, <articles.mercola.com/sites/articles/archive/2015/06/25/brain-immune-system-connection.aspx>.

Mesnage, R., et al. "Potential toxic effects of glyphosate and its commercial formulations below regulatory limits", *Food and Chemical Toxicology*, vol. 84, October 2015, pp. 133-153. Accessed 18 December 2016, <www.sciencedirect.com/science/article/pii/S027869151530034X>.

National Heart, Lung, and Blood Institute and Boston University, Framingham Heart Study. n.d. Accessed 5 March 2017, <www.framinghamheartstudy.org>.

Okereke, Olivia, et al. "Dietary fat types and 4-year cognitive change in community-dwelling older women", *Annals of Neurology*, vol. 72, no. 1, 2012, pp. 124-134. Accessed 11 December 2016, <www.ncbi.nlm.nih.gov/pmc/articles/PMC3405188>.

Parameswaran, K. and S. Sadasivam. "Changes in the carbohydrates and nitrogenous components during germination of proso millet, Panicum miliaceum", vol. 45, no. 2, 1994, pp. 97-102. Accessed 11 December 2016, <www.ncbi.nlm.nih.gov/pubmed/8153070>.

Peters, S., et al. "Randomised clinical trial: gluten may cause depression in subjects with non-coeliac gluten sensitivity – an exploratory clinical study", *Alimentary Pharmacology and Therapeutics*, vol. 39, no. 10, 2014, pp. 1104-1112. Accessed 11 December 2016, <www.ncbi.nlm.nih.gov/pubmed/24689456>.

Relationships Australia. "What is Coercive Control?", 23 April, 2021. Accessed April 26, 2022, Relationships Australia, Queensland: https://www.raq.org.au/blog/what-coercive-control.

Saatcioglu, Fahri. "Regulation of gene expression by yoga, meditation and related practices: a review of recent studies", *Asian Journal of Psychiatry*, vol. 6, no. 1, 2013, pp. 74-77. Accessed 28 December 2016, <www.sciencedirect.com/science/article/pii/S1876201812001931>.

Schucman, H. and W. Thetford. *A Course in Miracles*. Foundation for Inner Peace, 1992.

U.S. National Library of Medicine. "MTHFR gene", Genetics Home Reference, n.d. Accessed 28 February 2017, <ghr.nlm.nih.gov/gene/MTHFR>.

Victoria Museum. "Bread", Scientists & Discovery, n.d. Accessed 5 December 2016, <museumvictoria.com.au/scidiscovery/chemicals/bread.asp>.

World Heath Organization. "Who calls on countries to reduce sugars intake among adults and children", Press release, 4 March 2015. Accessed 18 October 2016, <www.who.int/mediacentre/news/releases/2015/sugar-guideline/en>.

ACKNOWLEDGEMENTS

I gratefully acknowledge my teachers and coaches as well as world teachers who have inspired me on my path: Jean Houston, Marianne Williamson, Caroline Myss and Oprah Winfrey.

Thank you to Candice and Diane, who listened to my theories and read my early drafts. To Dean, who read my early drafts and my final draft, thank you for your valuable feedback, wisdom and support.

Thank you to Eddie for reading my first completed manuscript, and for your absolute belief in me. Thank you to Marcie, who power read my first manuscript in one sitting, thank you for your faith, encouragement and love. Thank you to Sara, who read my manuscript in between teaching, for your support and loving joy. To Josie and my mother for reading my manuscript, thank you for your encouragement and feedback. To Indira for your valuable insight and wisdom, and to the great teacher that you are, thank you. To Andrew, thank you for power reading my final manuscript. To Renea, thank you for reviewing my citations and for your encouragement. Thank you to Ioanna and Laura for reading my final manuscript, for your suggestions and encouragement.

Thank you to Chris for answering my grammar questions. And finally, thank you to my editor Stephanie for her advice and final check to print.

Contact information

You can contact the author at her website: tamleerson.com, or on social media:

Instagram: TamLeerson.

Facebook: Breaking the habit of Dating Your Past.

Email: info@tamleerson.com.